DOCUMENTS OF MODERN HISTORY

General Editors:

A. G. Dickens
Professor of History in the University of London

Alun Davies
Professor of Modern History, University College, Swansea

DOCUMENTS OF MODERN HISTORY

THE DIVIDED SOCIETY

PARTIES AND POLITICS IN ENGLAND 1694-1716

edited by

Geoffrey Holmes
University of Glasgow

and

W. A. Speck
University of Newcastle-upon-Tyne

New York · St. Martin's Press · 1968

© Geoffrey Holmes and W. A. Speck 1967

First Published 1967

First published in Great Britain by
Edward Arnold (Publishers) Ltd

First published in
the United States of America in 1968

Library of Congress Catolog Card Number : 67-29569

Robert Manning Strozier Library

FEB 2 1978

Tallahassee, Florida

Printed in Great Britain by
Robert Cunningham and Sons Ltd, Alva

CONTENTS

	Page
Preface	xi
Abbreviations	xii
Note on Dates	xii
INTRODUCTION	1

PART I: THE COURSE OF CONFLICT

A. POLITICS IN 1694-5   8

    1 The Triennial Act, 1694   11
    2 A 'Manager's' View of the Party Situation, 1694   11
    3 The Composition of the House of Commons, 1694-5   12
    4 Opposition to the Bank of England, 1694   13
    5 Whig Divisions in 1695   13

B. THE CHANGING FACE OF THE HOUSE OF COMMONS, 1695-1701   15

    1 The Dissolution and General Election of 1695   17
    2 Court and Country in 1698   18
    3 The Uncommitted Country Members in 1700   19
    4 Whig Gains and Disappointments in the General Election of December 1701   19

C. POLITICS IN 1701-2   20

    1 Prospects for a new Parliament, January 1701   22
    2 The Election of a Speaker, February 1701   23
    3 Party Tactics on the Bill of Settlement, 1701   23
    4 The Impeachments and the Political Watershed, April-December 1701   24
    5 Professions of a new Queen, 1702   25

CONTENTS

D. THE CHANGING FACE OF THE HOUSE OF COMMONS, 1702-15   27

   1 The General Election of 1705   29
   2 The General Election of 1708   29
   3 The Court, the Parties and the October Club, November 1710-March 1711   30
   4 The General Election of 1713   31
   5 The Triumph of the Whigs, 1715   32

E. POLITICS IN 1715-16   33

   1 Tory Preparations for the General Election of 1715   34
   2 The Tories reunited in Opposition, March 1715   35
   3 The Tory Ex-Ministers under Fire, 1715   35
   4 The Tories and the Fifteen   37
   5 The Beginning of the Whig Schism   37
   6 The Septennial Act, 1716   38

PART II: THE CONFLICT OF PARTY IN SOCIETY

F. LONDON   40

   1 The Calves-Head Club, 1703   41
   2 Coffee House Politicians, 1705   42
   3 The Bank of England Elections, 1711   42
   4 An Aldermanic By-Election, 1711   43
   5 The Theatre, 1713   44

G. THE PROVINCES   45

   1 Party Spoils: Commissioners of the Peace, 1702   47
   2 Leicestershire, 1707   48
   3 Party Rage in Yorkshire, 1710   48
   4 The Corporations of Cornwall, 1712   49

H. THE CHURCH   49

   1 The Disputes in Convocation, 1702-3   52
   2 A High Church Martyr, 1705   53
   3 'A Dialogue betwixt a Bishop and a Priest', 1705   54
   4 High Church Clergy and a Low Church Bishop, 1706   56
   5 Party Patronage in Norfolk, 1706   57
   6 Pulpit Electioneering in Durham, 1708   57

	CONTENTS	
I.	THE PROFESSIONS: THE ARMED FORCES AND THE LAW	58
	1 Politics, Patronage and Promotion in the Camp, 1705	60
	2 The Harley Ministry and the Army, 1710	61
	3 The Disgrace of Three Whig Generals, December 1710	62
	4 Lord Chief Justice Parker and the Parties at Derby, September 1710	63
	5 Lord Cowper's Advice to George I on Judicial Appointments, 1714	64
J.	THE PRESS	66
	1 Illicit Reporting of Parliamentary Debates, 1694	68
	2 The Case for a Free Press, 1697	69
	3 A Newspaper Election Report, 1710	70
	4 Swift on the Resurrection of the Whigs, 1711	71
	5 The Politicians and the Press	73
	6 The Government, the Commons and the Press	74
K.	THE MOB	77
	1 Jacobitism in Drury Lane, 1695	78
	2 The Sacheverell Riots, 1710	79
	3 Disturbances on King William's Birthday, 1712	80
	4 Street Warfare in the Bristol Election, 1713	81
L.	WOMEN AND POLITICS	82
	1 Bedchamber Politics: The Influence of Abigail Masham	84
	2 The Duchess of Marlborough's Electioneering at St. Albans, 1705	85
	3 Women and the Sacheverell Trial, 1710	86
	4 A Whig Cameo: Ann Clavering	87

PART III: THE SUBSTANCE OF CONFLICT

M.	ISSUES	88
	(a) War and Foreign Policy	
	1 A Tory Merchant's Opinion of William III's Foreign Policy, 1701	91
	2 The Spanish Succession War through Tory Eyes, 1703	92

CONTENTS

3 Flanders versus Spain: The Commons' Debate on the Queen's Message concerning the Defeat at Brihuega, 1711	92
4 The Attack on the Barrier Treaty, 1712	94
5 Principles of Tory Foreign Policy after the Spanish Succession War	95
6 The Whigs and 'The Balance of the North', 1716	97

(b) Government and Monarchy   98

1 The Reception of the Association, 1696	99
2 The Tories and the Abjuration Oath, 1702	101
3 The Whigs and the Prerogative: The Standing Army Controversy of 1697-9	102
4 The Whigs and the Prerogative: The Fears of Queen Anne, 1708	103
5 A Whig Definition of the Right of Resistance, 1710	103
6 A Warning to the Voters of Cockermouth not to choose Whigs, 1710	104

(c) The Succession   105

1 The 'Hanover Motion' and the Regency Bill, 1705-6	107
2 The Pretender's Invasion Attempt and the General Election of 1708	109
3 The Tory Split on the Succession, 1713-14: Hanover Tories and Jacobites	110
4 The Commons' Debate on the Danger to the Succession, 1714	112
5 A Whig Paean on the Peaceful Accession of George I	113

(d) Religion   114

1 'The Church in Danger', 1697-1710	116
2 Occasional Conformity, 1697-1704	117
3 The Schism Bill, 1714	121
4 The Dissenting Vote	122

(e) Manifestos, Instructions and Addresses   124

1 Instructions to Whig Members, 1701	125
2 Professions of the Tory Faith, 1710	126
3 Robert Walpole's Address to the Electors of King's Lynn, 1713	129
4 Tory Manifesto for the 1715 Election	129

N. INTERESTS — 131

1 The Two East India Companies and the General Election of 1701 — 134
2 Gentry versus Army and City, 1708-10 — 134
3 The Grievances of the Landed Interest, 1709 — 135
4 The Bank intervenes in Politics, 1710 — 136
5 Social and Party Divisions in Kent, 1713 — 137
6 The Country Whigs and Landed Qualification — 137

O. PLACE AND POWER — 138

1 Parties and Places, 1697-8 — 139
2 A Party Appeal to a Placeman's Conscience, 1705 — 140
3 Honest Tom Wharton refuses a Bribe, 1708 — 141
4 St. John on the Motives of the Tories, 1710-11 — 141

P. COURT AND COUNTRY — 143

1 The Court Party in William's Reign — 145
2 The Country Party in William's Reign — 147
3 Country Whigs in Anne's Reign: The 'Whimsicals', 1706 — 149
4 Country Tories in Anne's Reign: The March Club, 1712 — 151

PART IV: THE ARENAS OF CONFLICT — 152

Q. THE CONSTITUENCIES

1 Bribery, Browbeating and Corruption in Aylesbury, 1695 — 154
2 Whig Organisation in Dorset and Wiltshire, 1701 — 156
3 Tory Organisation in Gloucestershire, Northamptonshire and Warwickshire, 1702 — 156
4 Lord Wharton's Electoral Empire — 157
5 Yorkshire, 1710: Canvassing Notes of a Tory Candidate's Agent — 158

R. PARLIAMENT — 160

1 Supply and Grievances in 1697 — 162
2 Party Tactics in Both Houses, 1703 — 162
3 Whig Preparations in the Summer Recess, 1707 — 163
4 Tory Preparations for the Opening of Parliament, 1708 — 163

	5 The October Club and the Leather Duty, 1711	164
	6 Tory Whips in the House of Lords, 1712	166
S.	COURT AND COUNCIL	166
	1 The King's Manager: Lord Sunderland and the Whigs, 1695	169
	2 Cabinet and Council divided over the Dissolution of Parliament, 1701	170
	3 The Debate in the Privy Council on the Declaration of War, 1702	171
	4 The Duke of Somerset and the Cabinet, 1703	171
	5 Lord Nottingham's Ultimatum and the Fall of the High Tories, 1704	172
	6 The Crisis in the Cabinet and the Fall of Harley, 1708	173
	7 The Whig Junto and the Cabinet, 1708-9	174
	8 Vryberg's Memorial, 1710	175
	9 The Privy Council and Anne's Last Illness	176
	10 George I and the Parties, 1714	177
	11 The Reversionary Interest: The Prince of Wales and the Tories, 1716	178

PREFACE

In a relatively brief book we could not possibly present documents illustrative of every aspect of political life in the years 1694-1716. We have therefore concentrated on what seemed to us to be the major theme of that period – the struggle between Tory and Whig, as it developed in Parliament and in parliamentary elections, in government, and not least in society at large. Such concentration must produce some distortion, as we are only too aware, in that it plays down or ignores certain aspects of politics under William III and Anne, for instance the nuances in the relationships between those monarchs and the politicians. We hope nevertheless that our selection presents a fair reflection of the essentials of our chosen theme.

Considerations of space also dictated one other important decision: the omission of several statutes which are relevant to our theme but which have become familiar features of every standard selection of constitutional documents covering the later Stuart period. We thought it more valuable to print material not readily accessible to students than to indulge in tedious reiteration of the clauses of such measures as the Bank of England Act, the Act of Settlement, the Regency Act, the Qualifications Act or the Riot Act.

The final form of our selection owes much to the kindness of owners and curators of documents in consenting to their publication. We are grateful to the Duke of Devonshire and the Trustees of the Chatsworth Settlement, the Duke of Marlborough, the Duke of Northumberland, the Duke of Portland, the Marquess of Bath, the Marquess of Cholmondeley, the Earl of Dartmouth, the Earl of Lonsdale, Lord Egremont and Lord Hampton, who kindly permitted us to publish documents from their family archives; and we are similarly indebted to Sir John Carew-Pole, Bt., Sir Gyles Isham, Bt., Sir Richard Hamilton, Bt., Mrs. Annette Bagot and Colonel R. E. Myddleton. We wish to thank the Wake Trustees, the Keeper of Western MSS. at the Bodleian Library, the Librarian of the University of Durham, and the Curator of Historical Records at the Scottish Record Office for allowing us to publish papers in their care. The editor of *Archaeologia Aeliana* also obliged us by authorising the publication of a letter previously printed in that periodical.

March, 1967

G.S.H.
W.A.S.

ABBREVIATIONS

Add. MSS.	Additional Manuscripts, British Museum.
Coxe, *Walpole*	William Coxe, *Memoirs of the Life and Administration of Sir Robert Walpole* (1798).
Hist. MSS. Comm.	Historical Manuscripts Commission.
n.d.	no date.
N.U.L.	Nottingham University Library.
Own Time	Gilbert Burnet, *A History of My Own Time* (Oxford, 1833).
Parl. Hist.	W. Cobbett (ed.), *The Parliamentary History of England* (1806).

NOTE ON DATES

Wherever ascertainable, dates are given in the Old Style, except that the year is taken to begin on 1 January instead of on 25 March

INTRODUCTION

On 22 December 1694 an Act 'for the frequent meeting and calling of Parliaments' received the assent of King William III (**A.1**). In the following October the Parliament which was responsible for this measure was dissolved; and from then until the Septennial bill became law in May 1716 (**E.6**) no English monarch could prolong the life of any Parliament beyond three years. The existence on the statute book of the so-called Triennial Act was largely instrumental in creating for two decades a unique political situation in England. In the space of just over nineteen years there were held no fewer than ten General Elections – six of them necessitated by the Act of 1694. Never before or since have English politics been so continuously subject to the fever of the hustings; never have English politicians been more thoroughly in the thrall of a growing and volatile electorate.[1] The traditional limits of the post-Revolution period, 1689-1714, have an obvious significance in dynastic and constitutional terms. But the accession of William III did not inaugurate, much less did the death of Anne determine, a distinctive phase in England's political development. In this field the real landmarks are the years 1694 and 1716.

Between these landmarks one persistent theme lends unity to the whole political scene. This is the struggle for mastery between Whigs and Tories. In the constituencies the theme is dominant throughout, save perhaps for one fleeting interlude (**B.2**). At Westminster it becomes more pronounced as the period progresses. Yet even there, except in the years 1697 to 1700 when its tones are relatively subdued, it always overrides the more intricate themes of post-Revolution politics, such as those introduced by the antagonism between Court and 'Country' or by the rivalry of connexions. Only when the Tory party is identified with Jacobite rebellion, denied by statute the chance of an early appeal

[1] The growth of the electorate in the 17th century, a development utterly basic to the emergence of national political parties in England, has been brilliantly illuminated by J. H. Plumb, *The Growth of Political Stability in England, 1675-1725* (1967), pp. 27-9, 34-47.

to the electors, and consequently deprived of all real hope of future power, does the conflict of parties at last become a subordinate theme, overshadowed in importance by the conflict of factions.

One of the most distinctive features of English history in the period of Triennial Parliaments was the involvement of the whole community in politics. It is true that the men who occupied positions of authority in this period – from officers of the Crown and members of Parliament down to justices of the peace – were drawn from a very narrow section of society (**N**). It is true also that what we should now call the political nation comprehended only the five per cent or so of the population which enjoyed the right to vote in parliamentary elections. But to visualise the conflict between Whig and Tory solely as a conflict within a ruling elite or within a privileged, enfranchised minority is not merely to misjudge its extent but to misunderstand its nature. At the height of the struggle in the later years of Anne the whole fabric of the national life was permeated by the spirit of party, to a degree without precedent even during the Exclusion crisis. Political history between 1694 and 1716 is the story not just of a divided Parliament, nor even of a divided electorate, but of a divided society. Party warfare both caused and reflected social division. While rival ideologies split society along Whig and Tory lines, rival social interests were championed by one party or the other.

To the apolitical and the uncommitted the England of our period offered a singularly uncongenial habitat. The social life and recreations of Englishmen, whether in London or in the provinces, were frequently invaded by the loyalties and antagonisms of the world of politics. The career of a professional man, in the Church, in the armed forces, and to some extent even in the law could be heavily dependent on the goodwill of influential members of the party currently enjoying political favour. The two most powerful media of communication in early-eighteenth-century England – the pulpit and the press – were also the two most effective instruments of party propaganda; and this propaganda was far from being limited in its impact to the political nation. Below the level of the electorate there was not merely interest in politics, in many quarters, but occasionally vigorous participation as well. Some of the fiercest partisans in Augustan society were women; and some of the most uninhibited supporters of the Whigs and the Tories were to be found among the unrepresented masses of London and the larger provincial towns (**F-L**).

Most of these features of the nation's life were decidedly more prominent in Anne's reign than they had been in the middle years of

William's. A divided society grew more divided as the years went by between 1694 and 1716; but it was about 1701 or 1702 that the rifts began to widen and deepen most conspicuously. It seems clear enough in retrospect why this was so. Society at large was responding to a polarisation of political forces at the centre; for in the years 1701-2 the pull of Whig and Tory loyalties became much fiercer in Parliament, in the administration and at Court (C). Not least dramatic were the changes which in these years came over the substance of party conflict. The major political issues of the day – above all those issues which evoked a sharply contrasting response from Whigs and Tories – were brought into far keener focus than at any time since 1689.

The crisis over the Spanish succession, precipitated by Louis XIV's recognition of Philip of Anjou as the rightful heir to the vast Habsburg inheritance, and still more by the French occupation of the Spanish Netherlands in 1701, played a major part in this process of redefinition. It served to harden the basic disagreement between Whigs and Tories over the nature of England's role in Europe, an issue which King William's war of 1689-97, and especially his methods of waging that war by a direct confrontation with French armies in the Low Countries, had thrust into the very foreground of politics. It confirmed the Whigs as the more outward-looking and the Tories as the more xenophobic of the two political parties in England; and hence it foreshadowed their disputes in Anne's reign over the conduct of the Spanish Succession War by Marlborough and Godolphin, and over the making of the peace between 1709 and 1713.

The events of 1701-2 gave life to old issues as well as highlighting others of more recent origin. Religious animosities, which had done much to sustain the first Whig and Tory parties of the Exclusion period but which had only been smouldering in the 1690's since the passing of the Toleration Act, now flared up afresh. From 1701 until 1717 they remained the most consistently divisive element in English politics. The conflict between the clerical high and low church parties in Convocation paralleled the secular struggle between the High Tory champions of Anglican supremacy and the Whig advocates of a fuller toleration for Protestant dissenters; and the irreconcilable nature of their differences did more than anything to preclude any genuine possibility of compromise or coalition between convinced party men, in church and state alike. Meanwhile the safety of the Protestant succession, the *raison d'être* of the old Exclusionist Whigs, had ceased abruptly in 1701 to be the matter for complacency which the success of the Revolution had temporarily made it (pp. 98-9). Thereafter, although legally guaranteed by Acts of Parliament in 1701, 1706 and 1708 (Acts which the Whigs enthusiastically and the Tories half-heartedly endorsed), it was a contingency that never could be taken for granted; and in the years 1713-16, when the latent Jacobitism of many Tories broke through to the surface, it became the dominant issue in the party war.

Closely connected with the succession issue was the great controversy over the basis of monarchy, the controversy between those Tories who claimed for the ruler a divine, hereditary right and the Whigs, who accepted only the validity of a parliamentary title to the throne resting on the theory of a contract between the king and his subjects. Logically this debate should have been rendered irrelevant by the acquiescence of most Tories in 1689 in the settlement of the crown by the Convention Parliament on William and Mary. But the history of the next quarter of a century was to demonstrate that the dictates of logic and the promptings of the Tory conscience could be two very different things (**M**).

The issues of principle which were at stake in the party battles of 1694-1716 imparted to the period a good deal of its distinctive stamp. But there was a conflict of interests as well as a conflict of ideologies between Whigs and Tories. Below the seemingly stable surface of the social order in the closing years of the seventeenth century and the first decade and a half of the eighteenth powerful rivalries were at work. One of the most startling developments of the 1690's was the rapid increase in wealth, and the corresponding rise in social and political prominence, of the businessmen – and in particular of the 'moneyed interest' of contemporary parlance. War and credit finance were the chief causes of this phenomenon; the Bank of England, the New East India Company and the stockbroker were its most unmistakable symbols. From the start there was a widespread resentment against the new rich in hundreds of manor houses up and down the country, where the families of the small gentry were fighting a depressing battle for their standards of living against high taxation and often low agricultural prices, being dependent for their income solely on rents. The Spanish Succession War, which kept the land tax at four shillings in the pound for eleven years while inflating the profits of the government's creditors, the City magnates and syndicates, severely aggravated these tensions. Just as the Tories, whose parliamentary strength was comprised overwhelmingly of country gentlemen, were the natural champions of the landed interest, so the Whigs, whose supporters dominated the privileged commercial corporations and whose leaders had close links with the City, became increasingly identified with the cause of the moneyed men (**N**).

Besides opposing ideologies and social interests, personal ambitions, as always, played their part in shaping the political pattern of 1694-1716. By 1714 almost 200 offices in the Crown's gift were in the hands of members of the two Houses of Parliament. The emoluments and perquisites of such offices offered a tempting prize to a generation which was bearing an unprecedented burden of direct and indirect taxation, the more tempting since this particular form of income was in practice largely untaxed. For some members, inevitably, the pursuit of place became an end in itself. But more often office was sought, by leaders and followers alike, primarily as an instrument of party advantage and an essential prerequisite of the achievement of party policies. An important corollary of this was a growing tendency throughout the period for placemen to take their cue from the Whig or Tory chieftains rather than from the sovereign and the Court.

It was ironical in view of this development that the years from 1705 to 1714 should have witnessed a vigorous campaign for Place bills – measures designed to cut down the number of placemen in the House of Commons. Such measures were promoted by the backbench country gentlemen in both parties, and were the classic symptom of that inbred suspicion of Country for Court which, at one time or another, had coloured the relations of all the Stuarts with their parliaments. But they were much more appropriate to the circumstances of William III's reign than to those of his successor's. For some years after 1694 a strong government party or 'interest' still existed in the Lower House. By the later years of Anne, on the other hand, it is scarcely possible to identify more than a handful of members of the Commons who could be said to make up a Court following, essentially independent of both Tory and Whig. The most effective antidote to 'influence' had proved to be party allegiance. Not surprisingly, the only major Court-Country issues other than Place bills to agitate Parliament in our period were virtually all (as with the standing army controversy of 1697-9) confined to the years before 1701 (**O-P**).

Within a society deeply divided over issues and interests and one whose aspirations and fears found expression in the competition of two national parties, triennial elections provided ideal hot-house conditions for the rapid growth of political organisation. By the early years of Queen Anne's reign Whigs and Tories were already organised for conflict to a remarkable degree both in the localities and at the centre. In almost every county of England and Wales where there was any likelihood of an electoral contest, and in scores of boroughs also, both sides had a recognised if not a permanent machinery for selecting parliamentary candidates and marshalling support behind them. Their methods were a strange mixture of meticulous planning and *ad hoc* improvisation: of practices (such as organised corruption or manipulation of the returning officers) that exploited the varied conditions of the unreformed electoral system, and other practices that were the precursors of the techniques of our own day. Yet their general effectiveness testifies to the reality of a local party structure between the General Elections of 1695 and 1715.

Once elected to Parliament the party man was in theory a free agent. But despite the absence within the parties of a universally-recognised leadership, a central committee formally constituted, or an official system of 'whipping', both sides contrived in some measure to harness and discipline the energies of their adherents. Parliamentary strategy and tactics were first worked out and then executed by teams of experienced debaters; and for major occasions in both Houses a heavy attendance could normally be secured by the Whig and Tory leaders (**Q-R**).

However, the conflict of parties in post-Revolution England was as much a struggle for the control of the King's (or Queen's) government as for the control of Parliament. The royal closet, the Cabinet Council, even at times the Privy Council were crucial arenas in this conflict. Consequently the monarch himself could never completely stand aloof from it. Even George I would probably have preferred to do so had circumstances permitted; and it is beyond doubt that his two predecessors were convinced that party was by nature noxious, and that they did everything they could to escape from its toils. Ideally both William and Anne would have liked to govern permanently through some form of coalition or 'mixed ministry'. But in practice such an object proved far from easy to attain. There were times (in 1695 and in 1700 for instance) when even William, for all his ability and his determined pursuit of his own political course, could not entirely escape the logic of a largely homogeneous administration. Queen Anne, equally determined but far less talented, was forced to accept something very close to government by party from 1708-10 and again from 1712-14. As for George I, though he did not wish in 1714-15 to exclude the Tories entirely from royal favour, he was powerless in the event to withstand the flood tide of a triumphant Whiggery.

Such success as the Crown did enjoy in preventing party rule after 1694 it owed in large measure to a tiny group of statesmen known as the

'Managers'. These men – the second Earl of Sunderland, the Dukes of Shrewsbury and Marlborough, Lord Godolphin and Robert Harley (later Earl of Oxford) – all shared to some extent the Crown's political ideals and were prepared to defy the party leaders, if necessary, to see them achieved. Their main service to the sovereign was to act as 'brokers' or intermediaries between him and the parties. It was they who supervised the construction of ministries and directed the electoral influence of the Crown, while under Anne Godolphin and Harley assumed full responsibility as virtual prime ministers for getting the Queen's business through both Houses of Parliament.

Indeed in many ways the Managers were the key figures in the unique political system of 1694-1716 – even more central in importance than Somers and his colleagues of the Whig Junto, than the old Tory chieftains, Seymour, Rochester and Nottingham, or than the new ones, Bromley and St. John. It was not least because the post-Revolution generation of Managers died out with the fall of Oxford in 1714 that George I succumbed so swiftly to the Whig supremacy, and that he did so even before the brand of Jacobitism condemned the old Tory party conclusively to the limbo of lost political causes (**S**).

PART I *The Course of Conflict*

A

POLITICS IN 1694-5

In 1694 the drift towards political confusion which had marked the previous four years received a decisive check.

The Revolution of 1688 had not been a party affair. Though the Exclusion crisis had divided the political nation into Whigs and Tories under Charles II, James II's actions had so undermined the privileges of the ruling classes that, whatever their party, they had withdrawn their support from him. After a compromise settlement, embodied in the Bill of Rights and the Toleration Act, the most serious controversies which had divided Whig from Tory, namely the succession and religion, were temporarily eclipsed, and the edge of party principle was blunted.

This was a development very welcome to William III, who was anxious not to become embroiled in English party politics, and determined not to yield his prerogative of freely choosing his ministers. His first ministry consisted of politicians who had previously distinguished themselves on different sides in the party struggle, Tories such as Danby and Nottingham holding office with Whigs like Shrewsbury and Devonshire. But the old differences had been too extreme to disappear completely. Even if all former sources of conflict had been superseded, men who had previously been bitter enemies would hardly have worked together smoothly. Personal animosities soon began to tear apart the fabric of government. William tried to patch it with a motley assortment of ministers, here a staunch Tory, there an Exclusionist Whig.

Before long, however, it became obvious that such improvisation could not produce stable administration, the more so because there was not only friction between personalities but genuine ideological argument. Although the immediate grounds of controversy had been overlaid in 1689, at bottom lay unresolved issues involving conflicting political philosophies (M). Sooner or later William III would have to choose between their advocates.

The decision was delayed because during the years 1690-5 the Crown enjoyed the seeming advantage of holding the balance between the parties. Since the General Election of 1690 Whigs and Tories in the House of Commons had been fairly evenly matched (3). But the attempt to trim between them only led to further confusion. The Earl of Sunderland, who emerged as the 'manager' between William and the parties in these years, advised the King to lean decisively towards the Whigs. William was reluctant to do so, particularly in view of the Tory association with the defence of the prerogative. The most celebrated of eighteenth-century Speakers recorded how he

> heard from a great personage that when the earl of Sunderland came ... to be in King William's confidence, and pressing him very much to trust and rely more upon the Whigs than he had done, the King said, he believed the Whigs loved him best, but they did not love monarchy: and although the Tories did not like him so well as the others, yet as they were zealous for monarchy, he thought they would serve his government best: to which the earl replied that it was very true that the Tories were better friends to monarchy than the Whigs were, but then his Majesty was to consider that he was not their monarch.[1]

This was the essence of Sunderland's sentiments when he wrote to the Earl of Portland, one of the King's Dutch favourites, emphasising the need for an approach to the Whigs (2).

Gradually Sunderland wore down William's reluctance. In 1693 the King began to make the decisive changes which were to identify his ministry more closely with the Whigs when he made Lord Somers Keeper of the Great Seal. This move towards the Whig party paid dividends in the next session of Parliament, for the votes of supply were crowned with the Act which established the Bank of England. But as William had feared, though the alliance with the Whigs brought undoubted advantages there was a price to pay. For one thing, party rancour increased, as the Tory landed gentlemen reacted bitterly against the new alliance between the Whig ministers and the City of

---

[1] *Own Time*, iv, 5: Onslow's note.

London, and pamphleteers like Briscoe, the Land Bank projector, exploited their fears (4). Furthermore the Whigs had demanded as part of their bargain with the Court an Act for triennial elections. The King at first refused to agree to this diminution of his prerogative, and vetoed a Triennial bill in the session of 1693-4. Then Sunderland insisted that to cement the union with the Whigs the Earl of Shrewsbury should be made Secretary of State, only for Shrewsbury to decline to take office unless the Triennial bill was allowed to pass. In the end William gave in, and in December 1694, eight months after Shrewsbury accepted the seals of his office, the Triennial Act became law (1).

The Triennial Act sealed the bargain between the King and the Whig leaders, but many backbench Whigs thought that it was too small a concession for a reversal of their traditional role as opponents of the Court. These old Whigs found in Robert Harley and Paul Foley a focus for their Country traditions. In April 1694 they showed their mettle by joining with the Tories to resist an attempt by the new ministers to foist a Court nominee on to the House of Commons as Speaker (5, i).

The collaboration of Harley and Foley with diehard Tories such as Heneage Finch and Sir Christopher Musgrave caused serious friction between the champions of the old Whigs and the two dominant figures among the Government Whigs in the Commons, Charles Montagu and Thomas Wharton (5, ii; also P), who along with Somers and Edward Russell, Earl of Orford, already constituted a distinct and formidable political group – a group later to become known as 'the Junto'.

Thus the distinctive features of the structure of politics in 1694-5 were these: a *monarchy* which remained deeply suspicious of party (as indeed did some of its subjects (3)), but which had at last been forced to come to terms with it; a *ministry* which for the first time since the Revolution contained a heavy preponderance of one party, the Whigs, and which relied very largely for its management of Parliament on a small group of ambitious, extreme party men, the Junto; a *Parliament* once more divided fundamentally by hostility between Whig and Tory, provoked by a new clash of interests between landed men and businessmen as well as by old ideological differences and personal feuds; a *constitution* which now made statutory provision for a General Election at least once every three years, a sure condition for the continued growth of party rivalry (**E.6**); but finally a *political tradition* of Country versus Court which was still sufficiently deep-rooted to ensure that for several years yet many Whigs would feel bound to oppose the government of the day on principle over a variety of issues, even if that government was in Whig hands, while some Tories would feel under an equal obligation to support it.

1 The Triennial Act, 1694

An Act for the Frequent Meeting and Calling of Parliaments

Whereas by the ancient laws and statutes of this kingdom frequent Parliaments ought to be held, and whereas frequent and new Parliaments tend very much to the happy union and good agreement of the King and people, we your Majesties' most loyal and obedient subjects, the Lords spiritual and temporal and Commons in this present Parliament assembled do most humbly beseech your most excellent Majesties that it may be declared and enacted in this present Parliament and it is hereby declared and enacted... That from henceforth a Parliament shall be holden once in three years at the least.

II And be it further enacted... That within three years at the furthest from and after the dissolution of this present Parliament, and so from time to time for ever hereafter within three years at the furthest from and after the determination of every other Parliament, legal writs under the Great Seal shall be issued by directions of your Majesties, your heirs and successors for calling, assembling and holding another new Parliament.

III And be it further enacted... That from henceforth no Parliament whatsoever that shall at any time hereafter be called, assembled or held shall have continuance longer than for three years only at the farthest...

Statutes of the Realm [1963], vi, 510: 6 & 7 Will & Mary, c.2

2 A 'Manager's' View of the Party Situation, 1694

The Earl of Sunderland to the Earl of Portland, 5 August 1694

I have so often repeated my opinion concerning the Whig party and the Tory party... but I must however say that the great mistake that has been made for five year together has been to think that they were equal in relation to this government, since the whole of one may be made for it, and not a quarter of the other ever can. Whenever the government has leaned to the Whigs it has been strong, whenever the other has prevailed it has been despised.

But as I have already said, I have endeavoured too often to show this, but though I have not been able to show it by the success of two sessions I dare be bold to say it will be very plain. I may be believed in this matter for the Whigs make me weary of my life, and I would give half of what I am worth that it were otherwise; and I wonder you and the King after so many years do not see it as it is.

N.U.L. Portland MSS. PwA. 1240

3 The Composition of the House of Commons, 1694-5

Anonymous letter endorsed 'For the King' [December 1694]

Considering the present state of the kingdom and the factions that are in it, the two great points that require more especially your care are how to manage the parties as to maintain yourself against the enemies abroad, and at the same time to preserve your authority at home, that the necessity of doing the one may not bring you to such circumstances that it will be impossible for you to keep the other; and this is more difficult because the Tories who are friends to prerogative are so mingled with Jacobites that they are not to be confided in during the war, and the Whigs, who are for the reason of necessity to be employed to support your cause against the common enemy will, at the same time, endeavour all they can to make use of the opportunity to lessen your just power; and, let them pretend what they will to you, the several instances they have given this sessions of their intentions that way puts this matter out of all doubt to any person who has taken the least pains to observe them; and it is beyond all dispute manifest, that they will give money to keep out King James, yet they never give you one vote to support your just right in any point where (what they please to call) the interest of your people is concerned . . .

. . . the most dangerous consequence of a new election is that it will throw the balance too much on the one side or the other, for either the Whigs will, according to their expectation, get it into their hands entirely, and then I fear you will think the impositions they'll be laying upon you unreasonable, or otherwise the Tories will have the ascendant, and then it's to be doubted that they, in revenge to the Whigs, will for the major part be governed by the artifices of the Jacobites, and from such a misfortune nothing less than destruction can proceed. Whereas, as the House is now constituted, the Whigs are not strong enough to make use of the necessities of your government as much as they are inclined to do, neither are the Tories numerous enough to resent your favouring the Whigs.

Calendar of State Papers (Domestic) [1694-5], pp. 363, 365

4 Opposition to the Bank of England, 1694

J. Briscoe, *A Discourse on the late Funds of the Million-Act, Lottery-Act, and Bank of England, shewing that they are injurious to the Nobility and Gentry, and Ruinous to the Trade of the Nation. Together with proposals for the supplying their Majesties with money on easy terms, exempting the Nobility, Gentry etc. from taxes, enlarging their yearly estates, and enriching all the subjects in the Kingdom, by a national Land Bank* [1st edn., 1694]

... I have, it's true, declared my opinion against the manner of raising money upon the late Funds, I mean of the Million-Act, Lottery-Act, and Bank of England; and I believe (when my arguments are well weighted) it will appear to be not without reason. I doubt few have entered into the account of it; but whoever lives but a few years will find them (if some methods are not taken to prevent it) like a canker, which will eat up the gentlemen's estates in land, and beggar the trading part of the nation, and bring all the subjects in England to be the monied mens' vassals.

3rd edn. (1696), Preface, p. 2

5 Whig Divisions in 1695

(i) Court Whigs, Country Whigs and the Speakership, April 1695

Mr. Wharton [Comptroller of the Household] stood up, and spake as follows: ... I am commanded by the King to inform this House that the late Speaker has sent him word, that his indisposition does so continue upon him that he cannot further attend the service of the House as Speaker: and further commanded me to say, that there may be no delay in the public proceedings, he does give leave to this House to proceed to the choice of a new Speaker. Sir, the filling of that Chair is the highest station any commoner of England can be called to; but, however honourable it is, the toil and difficulties of it are so great that I believe there is no reasonable man that hears me but would be rather glad to have it supplied by any man than himself: and therefore I shall, without fear of displeasing any person, out of so many who are qualified to serve you, to nominate —

Upon this he was interrupted by a great noise in the House, crying No, No, No; and several gentlemen stood up to speak to order. Exceptions were taken by several members, that it was contrary to the undoubted right of the House, of choosing their own Speaker, to have any person who brought a message from the King to nominate one to them.

Notwithstanding the Comptroller stood up again, and named Sir Thomas Littleton; which was seconded by Sir Henry Goodrick. Whereupon arose a debate: and another person, viz. Paul Foley, esq. was proposed by Sir Christ[opher] Musgrave, and seconded by the Lord Digby. And after a long debate, in relation to both the persons, the question was put by the Clerk, That Sir Thomas Littleton take the Chair of this House as Speaker. The Clerk declared the Yeas had it. The House was divided, the Yeas on the right hand, and the Noes on the left. The Tellers were appointed by the Clerk; viz. For the Yeas: James Chadwick, esq. 146. The Teller for the Noes: Colonel Granville: 179. So it passed in the negative.

Parl. Hist. v, 607

(ii) [Henry Guy] to the Earl of Portland, 14 June 1695

What you say concerning [Paul Foley] is true; but we must do as well with him as we can, and keep him easy in some points, since we cannot have him so in all. It will be a very hard matter, if at all possible, to get him ever to communicate with [Mr. Montagu]; for he says that he hath downright played him a trick twice, after a serious debate and a solemn promise passed between them; and therefore he will never more trust him. He says, likewise, that the most difficult point [the King] will have will be to have right persons for [management] in the [Parliament]; because he believes that the former [insolence of Mr. Montagu] will never be forgotten; and that behaviour made more uneasiness to several things than otherwise would have been; and that [Mr. Finch] and [Sir Christopher Musgrave] and several others have often told him so. He says that [Mr. Montagu] and [Mr. Wharton] do go about to [the Tory party], and assure them that if they will follow their advice, they shall find many things they desire to have effect. He is likewise positive that by a little pains [the Whig party] will totally leave [Mr. Wharton] and [Mr. Montagu].

[Mr. Palmes] was with me two hours yester morning, and told me that he had lately had a long conversation with [Lord Keeper Somers], who seemed much to despond because [the Whig party] were divided. He answered him that the sole occasion of that was [Mr. Montagu], who neither did understand himself nor would receive advice from others ...; that both [the Whigs and Tories] do generally contemn and laugh at [Mr. Montagu] ... I asked him what answer [Lord Keeper] gave him to all this. He said none at all; but shrugged up his shoulders, as a consent that it was true ...

I find from several hands, the violent [Whigs] do now despair of a [majority] to come up fully to them in [a new Parliament]; and therefore now discourse everywhere that this [Parliament] will be best.

> N.U.L. Portland MSS. PwA. 503
> [words in square brackets are in numerical code]

B

THE CHANGING FACE OF THE HOUSE OF COMMONS, 1695-1701

For several years after 1694 some confusion in the distinction between Whig and Tory persisted. It is some measure of this confusion that contemporaries found it very difficult, at least up to the end of the decade, to sum up the changing state of forces in the House of Commons in clear-cut party terms. This was especially so immediately after a General Election. By Anne's reign well-informed observers were able to compute with confidence, and often with remarkable accuracy, the numbers of Whig and Tory members returned to Westminster (**D**); the politicians of William III's day, by contrast, rarely attempted more than general impressions of a newly-elected House, and at times they were reduced to vague speculation and even to complete uncertainty at the beginning of a Parliament. Only by December 1701 (**4**)[1] do we find these mists finally dispersing.

The 1695 Election is traditionally regarded as a Whig victory. So, in a sense, it was; but as Bishop Burnet soon realised (**1**), it was a very qualified victory for King William and his Whig ministry – above all for his Junto ministers. Many of the members returned in 1695 who were ostensibly of the ministers' own party were prepared to support them to the hilt only in the vigorous conduct of the war. Under the influence of men like 'heavy' Paul Foley, whose re-election as Speaker the Junto was unable to prevent, some were even ready to join with the Tories in opposing measures which seemed likely to inflate the prerogative powers of the Crown or entrench the authority of a privileged clique at Court. These old 'country' traditions of the Whig independents asserted themselves still more strongly after peace had been made with France in 1697. Indeed the 1698 Election was the one General Election out of the ten held between 1695 and 1715 which was more of a contest between Court and Country than between Whig and Tory; and doubtless because the issues were so confused, both opposition and government leaders at first regarded the political situation resulting from this Election as unusually fluid (**2**). It was, admitted Lord Chancellor Somers, 'a nice question in what temper the session will open'.[2] And the subsequent division of the Whigs over the crucial question of the disbandment of the standing army (**M (b) 3, P.2**) was soon to prove his apprehensions justified.

This pattern of politics, however, was too freakish to last. Whig disarray after Ryswick inevitably played into the hands of the Tories, who were able to annex to themselves much of the credit for opposition to the policies of the Crown in the later stages of the Parliament of 1698-1700; and once William III began to readmit Tories in appreciable numbers to the ministry in 1700 the bipartisan Country opposition of the previous two years lost much of its relevance. It is true that as late as December 1700 an acute foreign observer in England could still

---

[1] The second of two Elections fought in this year.
[2] W. Coxe, *Private and Original Correspondence of Charles Talbot, Duke of Shrewsbury* (1821), p. 560; Somers to the Duke of Shrewsbury, 25 Oct. 1698.

identify a sizeable body of M.P.s in the Commons who were, in a very real sense, independents (3). Yet twelve months later, following the last General Election of William's reign, such a situation had virtually become a thing of the past. The same observer could now perceive only a triangle of forces in the Lower House, made up of Whigs, Tories and the Court (4). This was to remain the basic political pattern, with occasional variations, right up to 1716.

1 The Dissolution and General Election of 1695

The first point that was under debate upon his [the King's] arrival was whether a new Parliament should be summoned, or the old one be brought together again, which, by the law that was lately passed [the Triennial Act], might sit till Lady-day. The happy state the nation was in put all men, except the merchants, in a good temper; none could be sure we should be in so good a state next year; so that now probably elections would fall on men who were well affected to the government; a Parliament that saw itself in its last session might affect to be froward, the members, by such a behaviour, hoping to recommend themselves to the next election . . . These considerations prevailed, though it was still believed that the King's own inclinations led him to have continued the Parliament yet one session longer; for he reckoned he was sure of the major vote in it. Thus this Parliament was brought to a conclusion, and a new one was summoned.

. . . [The elections went generally for men that loved the present constitution. In many places, those who pretended to be chosen put themselves and their competitors likewise to a great charge; and everywhere there was more spent than could have been expected in elections to a Parliament that could not sit above three years]. The Jacobites were so decried that few of them were elected; but many of the sourer sort of Whigs, who were much alienated from the King, were chosen: generally, they were men of estates, but many were young, hot, and without experience. [At their first opening, the Court, seeing a great disposition in many to continue Mr. Foley, would not raise a heat by opposing him, so that he was chosen Speaker].

Own Time, iv, 287-8. [passages inserted in square brackets are from Burnet's original draft of Feb. 1696
(H. C. Foxcroft, *A Supplement to Burnet's History of My Own Time* [1902], p. 413)].

2 Court and Country in 1698

(i) Robert Harley to Henry Boyle, Brampton Castle, Herefordshire, 16 November 1698

The elections in these parts had nothing in them remarkable, but what, without doubt, you heard from better hands; and I have so entirely took the benefit of the country air that, notwithstanding the weather hath been very discouraging, I have made shift to divide my time between fishing, shooting and hunting. When I have been led out of my knowledge, I have found it for my safety to conceal I had been a member of the last Parliament. Had there been more time before the elections there had been many more changes: but though it hath much contributed to lessen the quarterly poll, even to a great sum, yet it is possible our Great Men will think that abundantly compensated by the change of the Chair from Mr. Foley to Sir T[homas] L[ittleton].[1]

The Court, it seems, are sure of this House, and others fancy fewer of the Country are left out than of the Court. When very much is expected or feared, generally the event disappoints both. If there be any alteration it will not proceed from the new members but from the change of opinions in some of the old, which it may be the general complaints and increasing poverty will oblige some to alter their measures.

Chatsworth MSS. Devonshire Family Papers, 102.0

(ii) Lord Somers to the Duke of Shrewsbury, 25 October 1698[2]

... I hope you will give me leave to beg your advice, what part to act upon the King's coming home. I own myself to be entirely at a loss what is to be aimed at. It is as yet uncertain what will be the temper of the Parliament. The elections were made on an ill foot; uneasiness at taxes, and the most dangerous division of a Court and Country party; so that there is reason to doubt of the behaviour of many of your best friends.

The King would in no sort declare himself before he went: I suppose,

[1] See p. 14 above.
[2] This version of the letter is an undated draft from Lord Somers's papers. The final letter, which differs significantly in wording from this draft, was published in W. Coxe, *Private and Original Correspondence of Charles Talbot, Duke of Shrewsbury* (1821), p. 560, where it is dated as above.

to see which faction would get the better upon the struggle. Whether he will not sit still upon the same reason till he sees the event of the session, it is hard to say.

Hardwicke State Papers (ed. P. Yorke, 1778), ii, 435

3 The Uncommitted Country Members in 1700

F. Bonet to Frederick III, Elector of Brandenburg, London, 17 December 1700 (transl.)

... Though the English are nearly all divided into Whigs and Tories, there are many country members in Parliament who have never joined with these parties to the extent of closely espousing either. These men speak and vote in the House according to their lights, which rarely reach beyond the shores of their own island. The principles which govern their reasoning are their care for

1. the religion of this country

2. the liberty of the individual

3. the trade which enhances the value of their produce, and

4. the cultivation of their lands.

No matter which is the party in power, and no matter how eloquent its appeal may be, it will never win over these members unless it can convince them that one of these four points is under attack.

Add. MSS. 30,000 D, fo. 363

4 Whig Gains and Disappointments in the General Election of December 1701

F. Bonet to Frederick III, Elector of Brandenburg, London, 16 December 1701 (transl.)

Prospects for the next Parliament seem good. Both the character of the members chosen so far and the majority of 30 which the Whigs have over the Tories augur well; and there is also the hope that 27 of the latter will lend an ear to the promptings of the Court and go over to the right side. This optimism will grow if the Whigs are given offices; but if the present Ministry continues, it is to be feared that it will prevail over Parliament, just as it did last year. It seemed astonishing that in the midst of the popular ferment against the Tories, whom many look on as the secret enemies of the state, so many of them should have been returned to Parliament. The best explanation one can offer is that the Tories had planned so well for the elections that they acted in full accord; whereas the Whigs were weakened by differences of opinion, and further divided by the different measures they have taken.

Add. MSS. 30,000 E, fo. 420

C

POLITICS IN 1701-2

In the course of the years 1701 and 1702 the pattern of politics at Westminster and the Court, so restless and confused in the late 1690's, settled into a firm and regular mould. Why these two years should have proved so crucial to the development of the post-Revolution parties is best revealed by a view in close-up of a number of their most significant features.

The first of the two Parliaments elected in 1701 opened with a contest for the Chair of the House of Commons which gave little hint of the developments that lay ahead. The candidates were Sir Richard Onslow, a wealthy country gentleman backed by the Whig leaders, and Robert Harley, who had the approval of the King and the ministry as well as of all the Tories. Even if the Whigs had been united behind Onslow Harley would still have won, for the Tories had a clear majority in the new House. That his victory was so decisive, however, was mainly due to the amount of Whig support which he was able to attract – some of it from placemen, most of it from backbenchers who still looked on Harley, with his 'old Whig' background, as a Country champion (2).

C POLITICS IN 1701-2

In the following December Harley stood again for the Chair. This time he received no more than a handful of Whig votes. The voting both for him and for his new opponent, Sir Thomas Littleton, was on fairly straight party lines. The transformation since February 1701 was remarkable, and its source can be traced back to three events which had taken place in the interim. One was the passing of the Act of Settlement, which named the Electress Sophia of Hanover as the Princess Anne's legal successor to the throne in place of the deceased Duke of Gloucester. Another was the impeachment of Lord Somers and two other leading Whigs for their acquiescence in the conclusion of the first Partition Treaty of 1698. The third, and most important in its immediate effects, was the crisis in Europe over the Spanish succession, following the death of Charles II of Spain, and the threat of French domination in both the Old World and the New which this crisis revived.

The progress through both Houses of the Bill of Settlement was a salutary lesson to the many Whigs who had voted alongside High Tories since 1695 on certain Country issues. It served to remind them that there were wolves concealed behind the sheep's clothing of their erstwhile allies. For although virtually none of the latter dared to oppose the bill openly, they indirectly obstructed it, or at least made their lack of relish for it all too patent (3). Certainly they showed less enthusiasm for securing the Protestant succession than for the vindictive attack on the Whig leaders over the Partition Treaty, launched in the Commons in March-April 1701. Ironically the impeachments of 1701, designed to break the Whigs by destroying their leaders, succeeded only in reuniting them and in endowing the Junto lords with a greater measure of authority within the party than they had ever previously possessed (4). What particularly disillusioned the Country Whigs was the fact that the attacks on Somers, Halifax and Orford were factiously pressed home at a time when William III was looking to Parliament to devote all its energies to countering French aggression, which was menacing English as well as Dutch and Habsburg interests.

Not every Country Whig perceived quite as promptly as the third Earl of Shaftesbury, grandson of the Exclusionist leader, the great gulf that separated Whig from Tory in their attitude to Europe (1). But by the spring and early summer of 1701 the whole Whig party was solid in its determination to support the United Provinces and the Emperor against the Bourbon threat; and after the prorogation of Parliament in June its local organisation set to work, by promoting addresses from all parts of the country, to convert public opinion to its views and to impute disloyal motives to the Tory House of Commons (4).

In the General Election of December 1701, as we have seen (**B.4**) the basic distinctions between Tory and Whig stood out more clearly than at any time since 1689. If the events of 1701 had strongly emphasised some of the issues which gave these distinctions definition, those of 1702 brought others into equally sharp relief. Of the events of this year two in particular heightened the ideological barriers between the parties. One was the growing Tory outcry against the practice of occasional conformity to the Anglican communion by Protestant dissenters for the sake of office (**M(d)**, **2**). The other was the accession to the throne in March of James II's daughter, Anne Stuart. The second event brought relief to Tory consciences sorely troubled at playing fast and loose with the hereditary succession. It also re-established, after a depressing interlude of some 15 years, the old Tory ethos of the party of the Crown. In spite of the fact that Queen Anne's first two major speeches to Parliament (March and May 1702) contained strong exhortations to support the war, they also included passages which encouraged all Tories to hope that the new sovereign intended to be *their* Queen, as Charles II had been their King. The Tories felt sure that, once this unwanted war was quickly over, Anne would become the Queen of the Little Englanders, of the landed interest, of the true sons of the Church of England (**5**). For this reason and for many others, by the time the first Parliament of the new reign met in November the transitional political world of William III was already as dead as King William himself.

1 Prospects for a new Parliament, January 1701

The Earl of Shaftesbury to Benjamin Furly, 11 January [1701]

We are now in the midst of our elections ... By the sound labours of our friends I am in hopes things are so well balanced that a good Parliament will be chosen, even under all disadvantages which can hardly ever happen again ...

The only thing to be hoped and prayed for is that the Tory party may not be superior: for if but ever so little inferior, their numbers will be of service rather than of injury. For as it is said of water and fire, so it may be said of them, *that they are good servants but ill masters*; and as by principles they are slaves, so they are only serviceable when they are kept so, and their slavery and subjection is the only pledge of our freedom, or of the freedom of the world so far as we in England are contributors to it. And let our friends in Holland know their friends here, and take notice that it [is] that party that hate the Dutch and love France, and the Whigs the only contrary party that can now save them and England.

Public Record Office, 30/24/20/53

2 The Election of a Speaker, February 1701

L'Hermitage to the States-General, London, 11 February 1701 (transl.)

Parliament met yesterday. The King was present, but he spoke only to the Commons, telling them to return to their own chamber in order to choose a Speaker. As soon as they were assembled there the Marquess of Hartington[1] proposed Sir Richard Onslow. My lord Spencer, son of the Earl of Sunderland, seconded him; but Sir Edward Seymour, the Tories and a great party of Whigs supported Mr. Robert Harley, and it was he who had the majority, with 249 votes against the 125 cast for his competitor.

This new Speaker has the reputation of being a man of good understanding and great integrity. The Whigs have regarded him as one of their party; but those who opposed his election did so because for some time past they have known him to be on friendly terms with the Earl of Rochester, and also because the ministry supported and even proposed his candidature, from which it was deduced that he would be too closely tied to them.

Add. MSS. 17677 WW, fo. 152

3 Party Tactics on the Bill of Settlement, 1701

The Evidence of Lord Chancellor Cowper to George I

It must be confessed that the Act for the Further Limitation of the Succession to the Crown passed in the 12th year of this King [William

[1] Son of the 1st Duke of Devonshire, whom he succeeded in 1707; Lord Steward in the Whig administration 1707-10.

III], while the Tories were in such credit, and had a majority in the House of Commons. It is therefore to be observed that the true reason why such a bill passed in such a Parliament was: that the King having, by his own inclination and probably the advice of some of his old ministry whom he continued to hear, earnestly recommended that bill to Parliament in his speech from the Throne, the Tories, for fear of losing the King's favour, did not endeavour to reject it, but set themselves to clog it, and indeed render it absurd by some of the restrictions [on the prerogative] your Majesty is undoubtedly apprised of, and to show their contempt and aversion whenever it came on, except when it was necessary to be present in order to load it, and by calling Sir J[ohn] B[olles] to the chair of the committee for that bill, who was then thought to be distracted and was soon after confined for being so.

Thus that bill went through the House of Commons; and many there who had let it pass hoped that the House of Lords, where the Whigs had yet a majority, would, by disputing at least some of those restrictions which were most absurd and impracticable, lose the bill. But the friends to your Majesty's family were better advised. They took and passed the bill with all its faults and without any amendment, wisely depending that if they secured the main, the succession, whatsoever was absurdly and unreasonably annexed to it would, at some fitting opportunity or other, be easily laid aside; which, their opinion, has already in a great measure proved true.

An Impartial History of Parties [1714], printed in Lord Campbell, *The Lives of the Lord Chancellors*, iv (1846), 425

4 The Impeachments and the Political Watershed, April–December 1701

Henry Whistler to Governor Thomas Pitt, 20 December 1701

Since my last this poor nation has been in an hurricane of humours from the mob to the highest. Our Parliament meeting, the Country party proved strongest and did charge the Lord Chancellor, Lord Halifax and Lord Orford with high misdemeanours. But they had made such a high interest with the Lords' House that the Commons delayed their prosecution, and the Lords pushed on the trials and did make ready for the trial of the Lord Orford and the Lord Chancellor and appointed a day for trial ... The Commons demanded by conference to settle the manner of the trial, but the Lords did not concur with them but went to trial; and the Commons protested against their proceedings, and so the Lords voted them not guilty. This was just at the end of a long sessions when the money bills were all passed.

This matter hath made a feud that I fear will not die. These lords, as it is said, have made a great party to decry our new ministry, as we call them, and to pamphlet the Commons, and by getting addresses bad ways to make the Commons little in the eyes of the people. And they have carried this game on too far and have got the Parliament by this means to be dissolved, in hopes to have gotten a Parliament to their ends and put off the present ministry, and to re-establish the old gang that has brought us into debt and made themselves by the nation's ruin. But I believe they will lose all their design; for most of the members of the last Parliament are chose again, and many others as good, and as much as we can see and judge the [Whigs] will lose their point and the new ministry will carry it – and they are for the Church. But the Whig party has used all their industry and power to carry it, but will certainly fail.

Add. MSS. 22851, fo. 131

5 Professions of a new Queen, 1702

On the eleventh of March the Queen went to the House of Peers, attended with the usual solemnity, and the Commons being sent for up, her Majesty addressed herself to both Houses in these words:

My Lords and Gentlemen,

I cannot too much lament my own unhappiness in succeeding to the Crown so immediately after the loss of a King who was the great support not only of these Kingdoms but of all Europe: and I am extremely sensible of the weight and difficulty it brings upon me.

But the true concern I have for our religion, for the laws and liberties of England, for the maintaining the succession to the Crown in the

Protestant line, and the government in Church and State as by law established, encourages me in this great undertaking; which I promise myself will be successful, by the blessing of God and the continuance of that fidelity and affection of which you have given me so full assurance.

The present conjuncture of affairs requires the greatest application and dispatch; and I am very glad to find in your several addresses so unanimous a concurrence in the same opinion with me, that too much cannot be done for the encouragement of our allies, to reduce the exorbitant power of France ...

It shall be my constant endeavour to make you the best return for that duty and affection you have expressed to me by a careful and diligent administration for the good of all my subjects; and as I know my own heart to be entirely English, I can very sincerely assure you there is not anything you can expect or desire from me which I shall not be ready to do for the happiness and prosperity of England ...

[25th May] ... her Majesty made the following speech to both Houses:

My Lords and Gentlemen,

I cannot conclude this session without repeating my hearty thanks to you all for your great care of the Public and the many marks you have given of your duty and affection to me. And I must thank you, gentlemen of the House of Commons, in particular, both for the supplies you have given to support me in this necessary war, and the provisions you have made for the debts contracted in the former. Your great justice in making good those deficiencies will be a lasting honour and credit to the nation. I wish the difficulties they have brought upon us may be a warning to prevent such inconveniencies for the future ...

I shall always wish that no difference of opinion among those that are equally affected to my service may be the occasion of heats and animosities among themselves. I shall be very careful to preserve and maintain the Act of Toleration, and to set the minds of all my people at quiet. My own principles must always keep me entirely firm to the interests and religion of the Church of England, and will incline me to countenance those who have the truest zeal to support it.

A. Boyer, *The History of the Reign of Queen Anne digested into Annals* (1703), pp. 6-7, 41-2

D

THE CHANGING FACE OF THE HOUSE OF COMMONS, 1702-15

All but one of the six General Elections fought between the accession of Queen Anne and the end of our period ended in a clear-cut victory for one party or the other. Only in 1705 was there an indecisive contest, although in 1713 some element of confusion was introduced into the picture by a split in the vast Tory majority between pro-Hanoverians and Jacobites. For the most part, however, the face of the House of Commons changed with almost bewildering rapidity as the advantage shifted first one way and then the other.

In July-August 1702 the balance tipped strongly in favour of the Tories, profiting from the emotional reaction which accompanied the accession of 'a Church of England Queen'. Their superiority was at first overestimated. One supporter actually sent the glad news to Madras that 'the Church party carried three to one, and not a Mountague got in the House'.[1] Even so an actual majority of roughly three to two, and the capture of just over 300 seats, held the promise of a new golden age for the squires and parsons. Three years later the dream had faded. At the 1705 Election the more extreme Tory members of the old Parliament, who had voted in November 1704 for the controversial motion to 'tack' the bill against Occasional Conformity (**M(d)**, **2**) to a money bill, had to face the combined hostility of the Whigs on the one hand and the Court interest, directed by Godolphin and Marlborough, on the other. Although the 'Tackers' were far from being annihilated (**I.i**), the Whigs gained enough seats to restore equilibrium in the Commons; and by so doing they created for Queen Anne's Managers the best opportunity they were ever to have of keeping both parties in Parliament in check (**I.ii**).

The next General Election was held three years later hard on the heels of an unsuccessful Franco-Jacobite attempt to invade Scotland. The political climate was thus ideal for the return of what Lord Sunderland was to hail as 'the most Whig Parliament [there] has been

[1] Add. MSS. 22852, fo. 10: Sir Stephen Evans to Thomas Pitt, 1 Aug. 1702.

since the Revolution'¹ (**2, ii**). It is a striking reflection of the extent to which party allegiances had solidified during the previous decade that in 1708 political pundits felt able to calculate the strength of both Whigs and Tories in the new House with complete precision: indeed before half the results were in, some observers were forecasting, with all the confidence of a modern psephologist, what the final total of Whig gains would be (**2, i, ii**).

The year 1710 saw a remarkable rejuvenation of Tory fortunes, coinciding with a ministerial revolution at Court in their favour, engineered by Robert Harley. When the revolution was complete Harley advised the Queen to dissolve Parliament. The General Election which followed, that of October 1710, fulfilled Robert Walpole's prediction as polling drew to a close that 'the highest complement of Whigs in this Parliament will not exceed two hundred';² and when the new members assembled in November the Tories found themselves stronger in numbers than at any time since 1685. A majority of 150, however, proved a mixed blessing to the Tory party. It encouraged excess among the many raw young extremists now elected, who were deeply suspicious of a ministry far too moderate for their liking. Indeed in the early stages of this Parliament the battle between Whig and Tory in the Lower House took second place to a struggle between the Court Tories and the High Church backbenchers: the former skilfully marshalled by Harley, the latter organised as never before through the October Club – a formidable pressure-group which was by no means as loyal to the ministry as one of its leaders, George Lockhart, later professed (**3**).

This division was healed by 1712, when almost all Tories in both Houses rallied behind the new government in its great work of making peace with France and Spain. But once peace was signed in 1713 a far more serious schism occurred within the party, this time between the Hanoverian or 'Whimsical' Tories and those who favoured a Stuart successor to Anne. This schism proved a godsend to the Whigs, for whom the 1713 Election would otherwise have been a real disaster (**4**). For them, however, the day of final deliverance was at hand. A Tory party grievously divided even before Queen Anne's death could not hope to escape demoralisation in the months that followed it. The full price was paid at the polls in January 1715, when the Whigs ruthlessly exploited all their advantages of public approbation and official

---

[1] Brit. Mus. Lansdowne MSS. 1236, fo. 243: Sunderland to the Duke of Newcastle, 27 May 1708.
[2] Blenheim MSS. B.2-1: Walpole to the Duke of Marlborough, 26 Oct. 1710.

countenance. Even in dire adversity their opponents had a strong enough hold on many constituencies to emerge with 200 seats; but this still left the Whigs with a majority of 150, easily the largest they had known since the Revolution (5). The new face of the House of Commons, the face of triumphant, vindictive Whiggery, could look to the future with confidence. Within a decade it was well on the way to becoming the face of entrenched, complacent oligarchy.

1 The General Election of 1705

(i) Henry St. John to the Duke of Marlborough, 25 May 1705

By the last post the account of the elections stood thus. There were 385 members chosen; of these 125 are new, and 32 Tackers are turned out. Your Grace will not be surprised that so few of the last have been left out, when you consider that few men attempt such rash measures but such as are almost certain of being elected again, either by the prevalency of their party, or the absolute dependancy of their corporations.
Blenheim MSS. A.1-20

(ii) [Mr. Eyles] to the Earl of Portland, 27 July 1705

The lists of the members for the ensuing Parliament are not yet authentically printed, but your Lordship may please to know that by the nearest computation [that] can be made the Whigs and Tories are equal, so that the Placemen will turn the balance.
N.U.L. Portland MSS. PwA. 410

2 The General Election of 1708

(i) S. Edwin to the Earl of Manchester, Exchequer, 11 May 1708

To back the honest [Whig] interest we are in hopes of a very good Parliament. I the more depend upon it because the Tories and Jacobites are a good deal dejected upon the elections that are passed. 'Tis computed we shall be 44 stronger in the next Parliament than the last...
Public Record Office, 30/15/7, i.xiv.ix

(ii) Sir John Cope to Sir Andrew Hume, 22 June 1708

I hope you have recovered your late fatigue at the elections and that you send up those who are for settling North Britain upon the same

foot as we are here. We have an account that the [Scottish representative] lords are chose and am sorry I don't find my Lord Marchmont in the list. I don't think they are all of a piece, as you hoped and feared; but I hope with lords and commons generally well. I think we are much mended in South Britain, for by a moderate computation the Whigs will be 299, and our friends upon occasion, the Tories, 214.
$$\overline{513}$$

> Scottish Record Office, Marchmont MSS. Family Correspondence 1671-1730, folder 1706-10

3 The Court, the Parties and the October Club, November 1710–March 1711

(i) The Commentaries of George Lockhart of Carnwath [1714]

When the Parliament was assembled in November 1710 it soon appeared that there was a great majority of the Tories; and all the former little subdivisions of the two grand parties were united and made two opposites, viz. Whigs and Tories; and of the latter, so many were private country gentlemen, chosen with no other view than to serve the nation, that had they united and entered jointly into measures, they had no reason to apprehend a conjunction betwixt the Whigs and those who depended on the Court, being themselves more numerous than both of these. But alas, they soon fell into parties and divisions... Though it must be acknowledged that it was chiefly owing to the unaccountable conduct of the ministry, who not only neglected to confirm and establish the advantage which they had gained, but did many things to disoblige and discourage a great many who at first had very good intentions...

The Tories, in consequence of the measures they had resolved on with respect to Mr. Harley [the leading member of the new ministry], did establish a society, consisting of a great many members of the House of Commons, who being for the greatest part country gentlemen who used to drink good October ale at home, were called the October Club. These gentlemen resolved and engaged to stand firm to one another, and to meet weekly in order to concert measures, in which the minority should yield to the majority; and they first of all unanimously resolved to trust to Mr. Harley's management in accomplishing what they so much desired and expected ... And it must be confessed that the far greater part of this club did adhere firmly to their principles and engagements, acting the part of honest countrymen and dutiful subjects, and that to their interest and power Mr. Harley owed his being supported and capable to stand his ground against the many traps which were laid for him.

The Lockhart Papers (ed. A. Aufrere, 1817), i, 320-1, 324

(ii) Robethon to Baron Bernstorff, The Hague, [10] March 1711[1]

The party of the Octobrists is dominant in the Lower House. These are country gentlemen, so called because of their warmth and because strong beer is brewed in the month of October. These fellows have carried the day in several divisions against the Whigs and the Court party combined. The greater part of these Octobrists are Jacobites. The rest aim at living as their ancestors did, when England took no part in external affairs. All of them are weary of taxes and seek an early peace ... If by allying with the Whigs [Harley] could form a party stronger than that of the Tories, he would do so tomorrow. But the party of the latter (or of the Octobrists) is so powerful in the Lower House that it is to be feared that Harley ... may be obliged for his own security to give himself up to them and enter into all their schemes ...

Ono von Klopp, *Der Fall des Hauses Stuart*, xiv (Vienna, 1888), 673-4

4 The General Election of 1713

Reports of the Hanoverian Minister, Baron Schütz, September 1713 (transl.)

15 September

I have seen Mr. Cadogan [the Whig M.P. for Woodstock]; he was on the point of going into the country. He was with Medlicot, one of the

[1] This letter, translated from the French, records not Robethon's own views but those of Marlborough, with whom he had just had a long interview.

members for Westminster, a great Tory but one who, Mr. Cadogan assures me, is most zealous for the Electoral House. He believes there will be several Tories of this character in the next Parliament, but that the Whigs will number no more than about a third of the House.

29 September

I think you should be satisfied with the lists you have so far received of the election results until all the elections are over, and then I will send you a printed list of them which will be exact. Accuracy is something one can scarcely be certain of with those which have appeared up to now in the prints, since usually those which come out today correct those which appeared the day before ... Cadogan told me that there were between 150 and 160 Whigs elected to the next Parliament, but l'Hermitage (**C.2**) is of the opinion that more than 50 of them will be expelled from the House, because in the constituencies where they were chosen they had Tories standing with them, and these having the majority will declare their elections invalid.

Brit. Mus. Stowe MSS. 225, fos. 196, 207-8

5 The Triumph of the Whigs, 1715

(i) Progress report in *Whalley's Newsletter*, Supplement No. 70 [February 1715]

Total chosen, 495. Whigs 299; Tories 195; double return 1; Court Tories 12. Whigs chosen in place of Tories 144; Tories in place of Whigs 4.

Cited in W. T. Morgan 'Some sidelights upon the General Election of 1715', *Essays in Modern English History in Honour of W. C. Abbott* (Harvard, 1941), p. 172

(ii) James Stanhope to Lord Stair, Whitehall, 2 February 1715

Our elections have exceeded our own hopes, and men very conversant and acquainted in Parliamentary affairs assure me that so many Whigs have never been returned since the Revolution. I have seen a letter from the duke of Roxbrough, who is positive that we shall have thirty eight out of the five and forty which the country sends, and that the list of lords will certainly be carried without any alteration. Monsieur d'Iberville, who was with me this morning, will, I dare say, confirm to his court the account I give you of our elections.

Public Record Office, F.O. 90/14

E

POLITICS IN 1715-16

During the years 1715 and 1716 the pattern of politics was almost completely transformed by the eclipse of the Tories as a party competing for power and the disintegration of the Whigs into rival factions. The main causes of this transformation were: the General Election of 1715; the discrediting of the Tory leaders; the Jacobite rebellion; the Septennial Act of 1716; and the quarrels that broke out among the Whigs.

On the eve of the General Election of 1715 the old party lines were re-formed for the last time. All but a handful of Hanoverian Tories threw in their lot with their former associates when they realised that the Whigs were to be in possession of overwhelming power in the ministry (**S.10**). The indiscreet electoral propaganda of the Tories provoked the King to attack them in the proclamation dissolving the old Parliament (**1**). Tainted with Jacobitism and castigated by the Crown the Tories went down to their biggest electoral defeat since the Revolution.

Nevertheless they were still strong enough to have carried the party battles of the previous era into the Hanoverian period if their leaders had not been driven from public life. But though they held together in the new Parliament (**2**), they could never recover from their leaders' fall from grace. The Whigs determined to impeach four of them – Oxford, Bolingbroke, Strafford and Ormonde – for their part in bringing about the peace. Anticipating this attack, Bolingbroke fled, though Oxford, with characteristic phlegm, stayed to face his accusers (**3**).

By enlisting in the service of the Pretender Bolingbroke confirmed the impression that the Tories were crypto-Jacobites, and this was reinforced when the Jacobites rose in rebellion in Scotland towards the end of 1715. In fact the impression was misleading, since few English Tories were prepared to side openly with the adherents of the Pretender (**4**). Nevertheless they were markedly more sympathetic towards the rebels than were the Whigs. Even the few Hanoverian Tories left in the ministry resigned in protest when their Whig colleagues turned deaf ears to pleas for clemency towards convicted Jacobite peers. This left the Whigs in sole control of the central administration.

The Jacobite rebellion proved fatal to the Tories in a second respect. It enabled the Whigs to justify the Septennial Act (6) on the ground of necessity, to prevent the confusion that a General Election might produce in the unsettled state of the kingdom. This Act condemned the Tories to the role of an impotent minority at least until the next Election, which was not held until 1722, and by that time their prospects were hopeless.

Meanwhile, however, the old party alignments became irrelevant as the Whigs began to divide among themselves. Perhaps some kind of upheaval within the Whig ranks was inevitable as the long leadership of the Junto came to an end with the deaths of Halifax and Wharton in 1715, to be followed by that of Somers in 1716. Not all Whigs supported the Septennial Act. But their disagreements on that score merely threatened to raise the old distinction between Court and Country (P). What added a new dimension to the political struggle was the conflict that arose within the new Whig leadership between Townshend and Walpole on the one hand, and Stanhope and Sunderland on the other. Although the final breach between them did not occur until April 1717, when Townshend and Walpole left the ministry, it first came out into the open in 1716. During the December of that year Stanhope demonstrated his ascendancy in the Cabinet when he informed Walpole that Townshend was to be removed from the Secretaryship of State and transferred to the Lord Lieutenancy of Ireland (5). The Whig schism had begun.

1 Tory Preparations for the General Election of 1715

Sir John Perceval's Letterbook, 26 January 1715

The Tories and friends of the late ministry are very industrious to procure a majority of their party to sit in the ensuing Parliament, and were for a while sanguine, but now they apprehend elections will run against them. They have used very vile arts to alienate the minds of the people from the King, and proceeded at last to the printing and dispersing a pamphlet called *Advice to the English freeholders etc*[1]: which is full of sedition, personal reflections on the royal family, and notorious untruths, insomuch that a proclamation was issued promising £200 reward to the discoverer of the author.

[1] See M(e).iv.

1 TORY PREPARATIONS FOR THE GENERAL ELECTION OF 1715 35

It was not till now that the King withdrew the favourable opinion he had of the Tories, for he was inclined to think only the great men of the last ministry his enemies, and resolved to continue as many of them as would be contented to accept of the employments he offered them. But this flagrant pamphlet, with the secret whispers and lies spread of him, and the open struggle the Tories make to support the last ministry, and rescue them from justice, has so convinced his Majesty that there is a party in the nation really his enemy, that he thought himself obliged to issue a proclamation for calling a new Parliament in terms that might satisfy his good subjects what his opinion was of some men ...   Add. MSS. 47028, pp. 10-11

2 The Tories reunited in Opposition, March 1715

Entry in Sir John Perceval's Letterbook

This day [17 March 1715] the Parliament met, and Mr. [Spencer] Compton was chose Speaker. Some days after his Majesty gave his speech in writing to the Lord Chancellor, who read it to the two Houses. But the King said first in English a few words to this effect, that he had ordered his Lord Chancellor to acquaint the Parliament with his reasons for summoning of them.

As it was feared so it accordingly happened that those who distinguished themselves a little before the late Queen's death by dividing from the ministry, and were therefore called Hanover Tories, fell in again with their former party, and that on the first opportunity, which was in relation to the Commons' address of thanks to his Majesty, some parts of which not pleasing them, they joined the rest of the Tories in a question for recommitting it. But their united strength made but 133 and the voters against recommitting it were 244. The address was agreed on the 24 March.   Add. MSS. 47028, pp. 30-1

3 The Tory Ex-Ministers under Fire, 1715

(i) Viscount Bolingbroke to Lord [Lansdowne], Dover, 27 March [1715]

My Lord,

I left the town so abruptly that I had not time to take leave of you, or any of my friends. You will excuse me when you know that I had certain and repeated informations, from some who are in the secret of affairs, that a resolution was taken by those who have power to execute it to pursue me to the scaffold. My blood was to have been the cement of a new alliance; nor could my innocence be any security, after it had been once demanded from abroad, and resolved on at home, that it was necessary to cut me off. Had there been the least reason to hope for a fair and open trial, after having been already prejudged, unheard, by the two Houses of Parliament, I should not have declined the strictest examination. I challenge the most inveterate of my enemies to produce any one instance of criminal correspondence, or the least corruption in any part of the administration in which I was concerned. If my zeal for the honour and dignity of my royal mistress, and the true interest of my country, has anywhere transported me to let slip a warm or unguarded expression, I hope the most favourable interpretation will be put upon it. It is a comfort that will remain with me in all misfortunes that I served her Majesty faithfully and dutifully, in that especially which she had most at heart, relieving her people from a bloody and expensive war; and that I have always been too much an Englishman to sacrifice the interest of my country to any foreign ally whatsoever. And it is for this crime only that I am now driven from thence ...

Parl. Hist. vii, 54-5

(ii) Edward Harley's 'Memoirs of the Harley Family' [1717]

The elections being over, being at Brampton, my brother took me one evening a walking, and fell into the discourse of his whole administration and particularly that of the Peace ... which, said he, though the events in all human probability will justify, yet I foresee that the malice of those who have so often sought my life will, with the utmost rage, pursue my blood upon this account. That which is called common prudence might prompt me to avoid the storm that I see is falling upon me, but having thoroughly considered this matter, and not being conscious to myself of doing any one thing that is contrary to the interest of my country, I am come to an absolute conclusion to resign myself to the Providence of the Almighty, and not either by flight or any other way to sully the honour of my Royal Mistress, though now in her grave, nor stain my own innocence even for an hour.

He added there are but two ways for a man to die with real honour; the one is by suffering martyrdom for his religion, and the other by dying a martyr for his country. He added further, you are now going to London, and you will be solicited to persuade me to leave the kingdom; but let not your concern for me influence you in this matter, for I am come, by the help of God, to an unalterable resolution of abiding the worst that can befall me.

Hist. MSS. Comm. *Portland MSS.* v, 663

4 The Tories and the Fifteen

... in that time a great many Lancashire gentlemen joined us, with their servants and friends. It's true, they were most of them Papists, which made the Scots gentlemen and the Highlanders mighty uneasy, very much suspecting the cause; for they expected all the High-Church party to have joined them. Indeed that party, who are never right hearty for the Cause, 'till they are mellow, as they call it, over a bottle or two, began now to show us their blind side; and that it is their just character, that they do not care for venturing their carcases any further than the tavern. There indeed, with their High-Church, and Ormond, they would make men believe, who do not know them, that they would encounter the greatest opposition in the world; but after having consulted their pillows, and the fume a little evaporated, it is to be observed of them that they generally become mighty tame, and are apt to look before they leap, and with the snail, if you touch their houses, shrink back, and pull in their horns. I have heard Mr. Forster [Tory M.P. for Northumberland] say, he was blustered into this business by such people as these, but that for the time to come he would never again believe a drunken Tory.

Robert Patten, *The History of the late Rebellion* (1717), pp. 93-4

5 The Beginning of the Whig Schism

Secretary James Stanhope to Robert Walpole, Hanover, 15 December 1716

You will see by my dispatch to Mr. Secretary Methuen, of which I send you enclosed a copy, the alteration which his Majesty has judged necessary for his service to be made in the ministry. If I could possibly have an hour's discourse with you, I am sure I should make you sensible that the part I have had in the last step has been for my Lord Townshend's service. Every circumstance considered, I do in my conscience believe this was the only measure which could secure the continuance of a Whig administration ...

... if my Lord Townshend shall decline Ireland; and if, which by some has been suggested, but which I cannot think possible, he should prevail upon you to quit your employments, the King in this case has engaged my Lord Sunderland and myself to promise that his lordship will be Secretary, and that I, unable and unequal as I am every way, should be Chancellor of the Exchequer for this sessions; the King declaring that as long as he can find Whigs that will serve him, he will be served by them. Which good disposition his Majesty shall not have any reason to alter by any backwardness in me to expose myself to any trouble or hazard. You know as much of our plan now as I do, and are, I dare say, fully satisfied that I think it highly concerns me that you should stay where you are. I am very sorry that my Lord Townshend's temper has made it impracticable for him to continue Secretary. The King will not bear him in that office, be the consequence what it will. This being the case, I hope and desire that you will endeavour to reconcile him to Ireland, which I once thought he did not dislike, and which, I think, he cannot now refuse, without declaring to the world that he will serve upon no other terms than being viceroy over father, son, and their three kingdoms. Is the Whig interest to be staked in defence of such a pretension?; or is the difference to the Whig party, whether Lord Townshend be Secretary or Lord Lieutenant of Ireland, *tanti*?

Coxe, *Walpole*, ii, 139-40

6 The Septennial Act, 1716

Whereas in and by an Act of Parliament made in the sixth year of the reign of their late Majesties King William and Queen Mary (of ever blessed memory) entitled, *An Act for the frequent meeting and calling of Parliaments*, it was, among other things, enacted, that from thenceforth no Parliament whatsoever, that should at any time then after be called, assembled or held, should have any continuance longer than for three years only at the farthest ... And whereas it has been found by experience, that the said clause has proved very grievous and burdensome, by occasioning much greater and more continued expenses in order to elections of members to serve in Parliament, and more violent and lasting heats and animosities among the subjects of this realm, than were ever known before the said clause was enacted; and the said provision, if it should continue, may probably at this juncture, when a restless and Popish faction are designing and endeavouring to renew the rebellion within this kingdom and an invasion from abroad, be destructive to the peace and security of the government; be it enacted ... That this present Parliament and all Parliaments that shall at any time hereafter be called, assembled or held, shall and may respectively have continuance for seven years, and no longer ...

Statutes at Large (1735), iv, 675: 1 Geo I, St. II, c. 38

PART II *The Conflict of Party in Society*

F

LONDON

A political thermometer would have recorded a constant high temperature in the capital during the reigns of William and Anne. The frequent parliamentary elections, and the elections of the Lord Mayor, Aldermen and Common Council were always fiercely contested (4). In addition party politics mixed with both the business and the pleasure of Londoners.

Though the Bank of England was a citadel of Whiggery the Tories made a strenuous attempt to capture it in 1711. Rival lists for the Governor, Deputy Governor and twenty-four Directors were published by the two parties, and supporters were energetically canvassed. On the Tory side 'Dr Sacheverell ... not only qualified himself for voting by purchasing £500 [stock] but was very busy and industrious in soliciting for the cause'.[1] Such efforts alarmed the Whigs, who summoned every available qualified stockholder to town. Lord Hervey was even inveigled from the horses at Newmarket to cast his vote (3). But the Whigs need not have worried, for they carried their entire list by a handsome majority. 'Dr. Sacheverell received the most terrible mortification, for being come to the General Court the 13th of April to give his vote, and make what interest he could, one of the electors to whom he offered his list told him 'This was no Mob business', indirectly re-

[1] A. Boyer, *The Political State of Great Britain for 1711* (1718), p. 261. For Sacheverell see also **K.2, L.3** below.

proaching him with the tumults occasioned by his trial, and some other persons gave him worse language, and threw dirt at his coach; of which he made complaints to a justice of peace.'[1]

The spirit of party not only disturbed business in Mercers Lane and Threadneedle Street but penetrated into the leisure haunts of the capital. Coffee-houses were in their heyday, and in them polite society mingled with tradesmen and more humble citizens. Yet although their patrons mixed socially, politically they were strictly segregated in Whig and Tory establishments. Woe betide a Tory who stepped into a Whig coffee-house, as one of Sir John Pakington's friends discovered in 1705 (2). In Anne's reign there were even rival theatres. The Tories eventually appropriated Drury Lane, while in 1705 the Whigs built the Haymarket by subscription among their supporters. The Whigs had the best playwrights, however, with Addison, Congreve, Farquhar, Steele and Vanbrugh, though the Tories did all they could to claim Addison's *Cato* for their own when it was first produced in 1713 (5).

Addison and Steele were members of the Kit-Cat, a Whig Club founded about 1700 which met frequently at the Fountain Tavern in the Strand. Though it was primarily a social club it contained many Whig politicians, particularly those who supported the Junto. There were other, more narrowly political societies, such as the Tory October Club formed in 1711, and the Hanover Club of 1712-14 which, though it eventually included a few Hanoverian Tories among its members, was predominantly Whig. A far less reputable Whig society was the Calves-Head Club, which caused scandal by celebrating the anniversary of Charles I's execution with ghoulish rites (1).

1 The Calves-Head Club, 1703

The Secret History of the Calves-Head Club: or, the Republican Unmasked [1703]

... By [a] gentleman who, about eight years ago, went out of mere curiosity to see their club, I was informed that it was kept in no fixed house, but that they removed as they saw convenient; that the place they met in, when he was with them, was in a blind alley about Moorfields; that the company wholly consisted of Independents and Anabaptists (I am glad, for the honour of the Presbyterians, to set down this remark); that the famous Jerry White, formerly chaplain to Oliver Cromwell, (who, no doubt, came to sanctify, with his pious exhorta-

[1] *Ibid*, p. 265.

tions, the ribaldry of the day), said grace; that, after the table-cloth was removed, the Anniversary Anthem, as they impiously called it, was sung, and a calf's skull, filled with wine and other liquor; and then a brimmer went about to the pious memory of those worthy patriots that had killed the tyrant, and delivered their country from his arbitrary sway; and, lastly, a collection made for the mercenary scribbler, to which every man contributed according to his zeal for the cause, or the ability of his purse.

The Harleian Miscellany (1810), vi, 600

2 Coffee House Politicians, 1705

G. Bradshaw to Sir John Pakington, 1 May 1705

I stepped into a Whig coffee-house yesterday, where I heard the Tories censured with as much virulence and malice as Whiggish principles could furnish 'em with, and presuming to speak in their defence (for 'tis thought presumption there to afford 'em a tolerable character) I was told I spoke more than became me, and that they wondered any Englishman would defend the proceedings of the Tories this time of day, adding several reflections. I answered that to return scurrilous language for answers was no fair way of arguing, but that I was not surprised to see 'em take such freedom with gentlemen's characters of more worth and honour than themselves, for they might plead prescription for that practice. This alarmed them, but they being truly moderate let me come off with a whole skin to sing the praise of moderation.

Worcestershire Record Office, Hampton MSS.

3 The Bank of England Elections, 1711

(i) Lady Hervey to Lord Hervey, 7 April 1711

I am now upon my Lady Sunderland's couch, and the duchess of Marlborough by me, by whose order I write this second letter to beg you would come to Town by Wednesday night, and bring everybody with you that has any votes in the Bank. Thursday is the day of election, and she says it is a terrible reflection upon any body that can stay to see a horse race though there were but a possibility of having the Bank of

England put into ill hands by it, and if the Tories get the better (as they threaten) Mr. Hopkins says you may all make use of your horses to run away.
[P.S. 'Pray come away that you may have nothing to repent of. S. Marlborough'.]

> The Letter Books of John Hervey, First Earl of
> Bristol (Wells, 1894), i, 287

(ii) Entry in Lord Hervey's Diary

I travelled all the night between the 11th and 12th of April from Newmarket to London to choose Governors and Directors of the Bank *at the earnest request of the Duchess of Marlborough*.

> The Diary of John Hervey, First Earl of Bristol
> (Wells, 1894), p. 53

4 An Aldermanic By-Election, 1711

Tory Partiality Detected: Or, A True State of the Poll and Scrutiny of Broad Street Ward on the Election of an Alderman in the room of Sir Joseph Wolfe deceased: Begun the 13th of September 1711 and continued by Several Necessary and Unavoidable Adjournments to the 27th of October (1712)

... The managers on Sir G. N.'s side [Sir George Newland, the main Tory candidate], it cannot be denied, took an unaccountable liberty, and treated their opponents with great haughtiness and scurrility. They objected against most of the pollers of the other side, upon the most trifling and ungrounded pretences ... and obliging all they challenged to appear, they used them more like criminals than fellow-citizens ... Most eminently serviceable herein was that Scrutineer of theirs, who ... turned perfect Merry-Andrew, rattling and raving, and imposing silence upon all, my Lord Mayor not excepted ...

Behold, ye Citizens of London, your Chief Magistrate ... in a Wardmoot of your City, hooted, insulted, assaulted and saluted there ... with the modern serpentine hiss.

Tell us, ye Tory loyalists, when ever the Whigs (by you unjustly stigmatised as disloyal and factious) thus treated their lawful magistrates? Is this, O ye only true sons of the Church, your unlimited Passive Obedience and submission without reserve? Have ye ... forgot your late rampant and darling (tho justly censured and condemned) principles? Blush, if shame has not quite forsaken you, O ye canting hypocrites, that bind heavy burdens on others, shoulders, and will not touch them yourselves with the least of your fingers – Blush, I say, that it should become needful for any of the ruined Whigs or unfortunate Dissenters publicly to remind you of your duty, as they failed not to do by their quiet and passive carriage in the midst of all your outrages in these late proceedings. Either open your eyes and own your folly, or permit the considerate part of mankind with scorn and contempt to set your contradictory practices against your avowed principles, and readily to see the force of your own concession, that Nature will rebel against Principle. O Tempora! O Mores!...

But what ails these restless High-Churchmen of the Ward? (for of such we would be understood to speak). Something sure must be at heart. Speak out, ye mad Enthusiasts, and tell us what you mean, when you bawl for the Church, the Church. Is it not to reconcile our Church to the Gallican model and to make our Crown feasible to the Pretender? Deceive not yourselves, and be no longer deceived by masked Jesuits and French emissaries. The world begins to see the cheat. But let all in this Ward, as well as throughout the City, join hand and heart with the true lovers of their Queen and Country to choose such Common-Council men and other magistrates as may without private views or sinister ends promote the public weal and honour of the City, as well as of the whole nation; that we may all sincerely fall in with that seasonable advice of King William of immortal memory, in his last speech from the throne: that there be no other distinction heard of among us for the future, but of those that are for the Protestant Religion and the present Establishment, and of them who mean a Popish Prince and a French Government.

5 The Theatre, 1713

(i) Lord Castlecomer to Sir John Perceval, 28 April 1713

Mr. Addison's *Cato* has justly gained universal applause, and is reckoned the best Tragedy ever came out in any age or language. Such has been its run upon the stage that the ministry are at last forced to come into its applause, notwithstanding their efforts at first were in opposition to it. But now the word is given that Cato must either mean my Lord Treasurer or Bolingbroke, and the contention is which party shall applaud it most. There was a good whimsical passage happened to me at Court last Sunday about it. In the apartments I met Mr. Harcourt, my Lord Chancellor's son, and rallying with him in asking him how he liked our play: 'Your play, my Lord, 'tis ours', says he, 'or at least you will allow Cato to belong to us by reason Mr. Booth is one of us.' 'Very good', quoth I, 'take him, in God's name; you purchased him at the rate of 54 guineas, which Lord Bolingbroke collected among you young gentlemen at the play the other night.' 'At that rate, my Lord', says he, 'if your friends will give him 60, you may bring [him] over.' Upon which I observed that it was by no means worth our while; and further added they might make the best of their player since we had our poet, and bribe him if you can. And this, Sir, was our gay interview, and this is a specimen of our present humour, who shall have the honour of the play.

Add. MSS. 47027, pp. 57-9

(ii) William Wogan to Sir John Perceval, 30 April 1713

'Tis not unworth your knowledge that one night the Whig lords had one of the boxes, and the Tory lords the other; the first clapped all the play, the other sat very silent, but at the end of it Lord Bolingbroke called to Mr. Booth and presented him with a purse of 50 guineas. The Whigs, says he, have clapped, but the Tories give you this.

Ibid, p. 60

G

THE PROVINCES

Away from the political heart of the nation the pulse of party politics was irregular, sometimes beating sluggishly, sometimes racing. Thus in 1707 Swift, on his way back to London from Ireland, observed that political passions were only aroused by parliamentary elections, such as that which he encountered in Leicester (2). Defoe had made a similar observation in 1705. Commenting on Leeds, Wakefield and Sheffield, which were not parliamentary boroughs, he remarked 'frequent elections having no influence here to divide the people, they live here in much more peace with one another than in other parts'.[1] Yet five years

[1] Hist. MSS. Comm. *Portland MSS.* iv, 272; Defoe to Harley, Sept. 1705.

later the Sacheverell virus (*see* **K.2**) infected even these Yorkshire towns, and High Church and Low Church fought fiercely for control of Leeds Corporation (3). By the latter half of Anne's reign corporation, and especially mayoral, elections were frequently contested on party lines (4). Such contests add point to Burnet's observation in 1708: 'The parties are now so stated and kept up, not only by the elections of Parliament-men, that return every third year, but even by the yearly elections of mayors and corporation-men, that they know their strength; and in every corner of the nation the two parties stand, as it were, listed against one another.'[1]

So many local appointments were in the gift of the government that, as Abel Boyer observed, something like a national spoils system was in operation during this period, 'the places of trust and profit being here, as it were, in a perpetual fluctuation according as either of the two parties that divide this nation prevails'.[2]

This spoils system could make even the lowest rungs of the administrative ladder insecure. 'I am obliged to trouble you with a request', wrote Lord Landsdowne to Lord Treasurer Oxford in 1713, 'that one James Prideaux, the present postmaster of Camelford, may be removed. He is an inveterate enemy to the present government, has set me at open defiance these seven years ... and that Mr. William Carew, of the same town, a gentleman of a good family, nearly related to Sir William Carew [a Tory M.P.], and a man of good principles, be put in his place.'[3] Thus even local postmasters could be pawns in the party game.

But perhaps the most significant gauge of party strength in the localities was the composition of the commissions of the peace. Justices were regularly purged by successive Lord Chancellors or Keepers of the Great Seal in response to pressure from their ministerial colleagues. For instance, sweeping changes were made by Sir Nathan Wright, who succeeded Lord Somers as Lord Keeper in 1700. 'In the year 1701', Robert Harley was later informed, 'his late Majesty King William was pleased to command Sir Nathan Wright ... to add more than 869 gentlemen to the commissions of the peace in the several counties of England and Wales ...'[4] These changes were made in favour of the Whigs. After Anne's accession there was another purge in 1702, when the Whigs of 1701 were replaced with Tories, some of whom had not even

---

[1] *Own Time*, vi, 224.
[2] A. Boyer, *The Political State of Great Britain for 1711* (1718), p. 275.
[3] Hist. MSS. Comm. *Portland MSS.* v, 306-7: Lansdowne to Oxford, 20 July 1713.
[4] Brit. Mus. Loan 29/29/11; petition of Thomas Edwards to Lord Oxford, n.d.

G THE PROVINCES

taken the oaths in the previous reign (**I**). This quickly transmitted the political upheaval which occurred at the centre in the years 1701-2 (**C**) to the remotest parts of the country. In 1705 Defoe observed how 'in all parts the greatest hindrances to the forming the people into moderation and union among themselves, next to the clergy, are the justices. Wherever there happen to be moderate justices the people live easy, and the parsons have the less influence, but the conduct of the justices in most parts is intolerably scandalous, especially in Wilts, in Lancashire, in Nottingham, Leicester, Warwick, Northampton, Suffolk, Essex and Middlesex.'[1] That Defoe was justified in considering the clergy to be even worse will readily be seen from the next section (**H**).

1 Party Spoils: Commissioners of the Peace, 1702

The Duke of Devonshire to the Duke of Somerset, 3 August 1702

Before I had the honour of your Grace's of the last post I had the dissatisfaction not to find in the *Gazette* the names of those persons whom your interest brought into the last Parliament, and indeed generally the list of the new members (as far as I have seen) does not afford a very pleasing prospect. I wish your endeavours in other places had been as successful as they were to my son in Yorkshire, whose election there is so much owing to your Grace. I have had an answer from my Lord Keeper [Wright] much to the same purpose of that he gave your Grace, with this addition, that in his opinion those who would never own the government in the last reign are very fit to be employed if they will own it in this. His Lordship's notion seems a little extraordinary, since 'tis hard to conceive what objection they could have to the establishment in the last reign, that does not remain the same in this. I am not so much concerned at his overlooking me (tho' custos [rotulorum] for this county) but that really he has left out some of the usefullest men, and that indeed cannot well be spared, and put in Jacobites, or men of no estates, and that have nothing to recommend them, but that they are violently of a party. But finding from what your Grace intimates, as well as from other hands, that his practice has been the same in most places, I shall give his Lordship no farther trouble at present but wait for a fitter opportunity.

Alnwick Castle MSS. vol. 21 i, fo. 176

[1] Hist. MSS. Comm. *Portland MSS.* iv, 272; Defoe to Harley, Oct. 1705.

2 Leicestershire, 1707

Jonathan Swift to Archbishop King, Leicester, 6 December 1707

This long war has here occasioned no fall [in the price] of lands, nor much poverty among any sort of people; only some complain of a little slowness in tenants to pay their rents, more than formerly. There is a universal love of the present government, and few animosities except upon elections, of which I just arrived to see one in this town upon a vacancy by the death of a knight of the shire. They have been polling these three days, and the number of thousands pretty equal on both sides: the parties, as usual, High and Low, and there is not a chambermaid, prentice, or schoolboy in this whole town but what is warmly engaged on one side or the other.

The Correspondence of Jonathan Swift (ed. F. Elrington Ball, 1910), i, 38-9

3 Party Rage in Yorkshire, 1710

Ralph Thoresby to John Strype, Leeds, 16 October 1710 [copy]

... This wretched ferment yet continues here. Mr. Lowther is thrown out at Pontefract (though 'tis said by foul play, as my cousin Lee was also from being mayor there), and 'tis doubtful Sir W[illia]m Strickland will have the same fate in the county. We have succeeded better (as to the Recordership) in this town, and have got in my nephew Wilson to be Recorder by a great majority of votes, the opponent having but 5. Yet I am told to my face that if he had but 2 votes, he shall stand. Because of the present ferment they hope to prevail for the royal approbation, by making a representation as false as it is scandalous to the Court, as though the Corporation was desperately Whiggish. Whereas there is but one person, or two at the most, that ever go, so much as occasionally, to the [Dissenting] meetings. But whoever is not a Sacheverellite is so reputed; and they cannot bear that the governing part of the town, as well as the generality of the commoners, should be moderate.

Add. MSS. 5853, fo. 88

4 The Corporations of Cornwall, 1712

Lord Lansdowne to Lord Oxford, 30 September 1712

Mr. Vincent and his son are going post tomorrow for Cornwall to be present at the election of a mayor for the town of Truro, where we are in danger, or rather under a certainty, of losing both members at the next choice for a Parliament, unless your Lordship is pleased to give your assistance. I have appropriated every penny of my own rents in that county for services of this kind, being attacked in every corporation. It is not to be imagined what efforts have been made, and what money has been lavished upon this occasion. The contention and expense is greater than ever was known upon the choice of a Parliament, so much the enemies of the Government have thought it necessary to be before hand with us in securing the returning officers.

Hist. MSS. Comm. *Portland MSS.* v, 229

H

THE CHURCH

Few political developments did more to divide English society during the period 1694-1716 than the emergence of High Church and Low Church parties amongst the clergy. In general this split separated the bulk of the inferior clergy, who were inclined to the High Church party, from their superiors, particularly the bishops, most of whom took the Low Church side. These parties were the ecclesiastical counterparts of the Tory and Whig parties.

William III is often held responsible for creating this division, by choosing Low Church clergymen to fill the many vacancies which occurred in the upper ranks of the hierarchy immediately after the Revolution. The true nature of these initial appointments in the Church, which has only recently been clarified, was very different. They were made not in consultation with the Whigs, but on the advice of the

Tory Earl of Nottingham.[1] Despite his Whig bias Bishop Burnet was not far off the mark when he wrote that 'soon after the Revolution some great preferments had been given among them [the High Church clergy]: but it appearing that they were soured with a leaven that had gone too deep to be wrought out, a stop was put to the courting them any more'.[2]

This crucial change in ecclesiastical policy took place not in 1689 but in 1694. When Archbishop Tillotson died in that year Nottingham recommended Stillingfleet as his successor. By this time, however, the Tory statesman had left the ministry and William was in league with the Whigs, who pushed the claims of an ally, Thomas Tenison. Although Queen Mary interceded on behalf of Nottingham's nominee, Tenison was promoted to Canterbury. Whatever moderating influence Mary might have exercised over Church appointments came to an end when she died in December 1694. For the next few years preferment went to Whig churchmen.

'When they saw preferments went in another channel', continued Burnet's account of the High Church clergy, 'they set up a complaint over England of the want of Convocations.'[3] The Whigs resolutely opposed the summoning of Convocation in response to these demands. But in 1701, when they came into power, the Tories insisted that the traditional representative body of the clergy should assemble, and it met for the first time since 1689. From 1701 until 1717 Convocation held sessions coincidently with Parliament, except between 1708 and 1710, when the Whigs kept it continually prorogued.

No other event in the crowded last months of William's reign did more to poison the political atmosphere than the summoning of Convocation. From the first its sessions were marked by the most acrimonious wrangling between the majority of the bishops in the Upper House and the majority of the inferior clergy in the Lower, who were given moral support by the lay Tories both in the Commons and in the ministry; and it was at this stage, Burnet tells us, that the terms High and Low Church, with all their political as well as religious connotations, became widely current (1).

As a Bishop very much in the thick of the political fight Burnet's testimony is most valuable. Nevertheless his Whig bias clouds his judgement of the disputes within the Church. The extent of his Whiggery can be gauged from the pages of a diary kept by Thomas

---

[1] G. V. Bennett, 'King William III and the Episcopate', *Essays in Modern Church History in Memory of Norman Sykes* (ed. G. V. Bennett and J. D. Walsh, 1966), pp. 104-22.
[2] *Own Time*, iv, 458-9.   [3] *Ibid*, p. 459.

H THE CHURCH   51

Naish, a clergyman in Burnet's diocese of Salisbury (4). In the entry for 13 February 1702, for instance, Naish recorded how his support for the Tory candidates for Wiltshire in the recent General Election had so incensed Burnet that the bishop had deprived him of the post of surrogate to the Dean of Salisbury.

But Naish's sufferings in the High Church cause were a trifle in comparison with those which Samuel Wesley endured for his advocacy of the same cause in Lincolnshire. In 1705 the evangelist's father was deprived of the chaplaincy of a regiment and hounded to a debtor's cell in Lincoln castle by the Whigs. His appeal to the newly-appointed Low Church Bishop Wake (2) fell on deaf ears, and he was eventually bailed out by subscriptions from High Church clergymen.

The relations between Naish and Burnet, and Wesley and Wake, were not untypical of those which prevailed between the bishop and the inferior clergy in most dioceses in England. Durham was an exception, for Bishop Crewe was a Tory, as a Low Church clergyman found out to his cost after the 1705 election in Northamptonshire, to the delight of the narrator, the High Church vicar of Daventry (3). Crewe not only backed the Tory knights of the shire in Northampton, but fully approved the support given by his own cathedral clergy to Thomas Conyers, a Tory candidate in Durham City in 1708 (6). Politics and perdition were often linked in sermons inveighing against the Whigs, which made the pulpit an invaluable agent of propaganda for the Tory party.

The activities of the High Church clergy on behalf of Tory candidates could have considerable effect (**J.3**). Defoe claimed that in 1705 'of 318 parsons in the county of Kent, above 250 of them . . . gave their votes for Sir C[holmley] D[ering], [a Tory]'.[1] At the Lincolnshire election of 1710 'the clergy marched in a body to the number of about 150' to vote for the Tories.[2] This 'Tory-Roryism' of the lower clergy put the Whigs at a serious disadvantage in the counties, which explains why Walpole's friend Sir Charles Turner was so concerned to get 'an honest parson' in a Norfolk living by taking advantage of his party's political supremacy in 1706 (5). The manipulation of Church patronage, indeed, was a long-term answer to Whig difficulties. When they came to power after the death of Anne they found the short-term solution in the suppression of Convocation, which was dissolved in 1717 and, save for one brief interlude in the 1740's, never met again until the mid-nineteenth century. The removal of this national sounding board for

[1] *A Review of the Affairs of France*, 29 May 1705.
[2] Brit. Mus. Loan 29/321. Dyer's Newsletter, 19 Oct. 1710.

High Church hysteria brought to an end a period in which the Established Church had been at the very centre of party political strife.

1 The Disputes in Convocation, 1702-3

The proceedings of the Convocation, which sat at the same time [as Parliament], are next to be related. At the first opening of it, there was a contest between the two houses that lasted some days, concerning an address to the Queen. The lower house intended to cast some reflections on the former reign, in imitation of what the House of Commons had done, and these were worded so invidiously, that most of the bishops were pointed at by them. But the upper house refusing to concur, the lower house receded, and so they both agreed in a very decent address. The Queen received it graciously, promising all favour and protection to the church, and exhorting them all to peace and union among themselves. After this, the lower house made an address to the bishops, that they might find an expedient for putting an end to those disputes that had stopped the proceedings of former Convocations. The bishops resolved to offer them all that they could, without giving up their character and authority; so they made a proposition, that, in the intervals of sessions, the lower house might appoint committees to prepare matters, and when business was brought regularly before them, that the archbishop should so order the prorogations that they might have convenient and sufficient time to sit and deliberate about it. This fully satisfied many of that body. But the majority thought this kept the matter still in the archbishop's power, as it was indeed intended it should, so they made another application to the bishops ...

From these disputes in Convocation, divisions ran through the whole body of the clergy, and to fix these, new names were found out. They were distinguished by the names of *High Church* and *Low Church*. All that treated the dissenters with temper and moderation, and were for residing constantly at their cures, and for labouring diligently in them; that expressed a zeal against the Prince of Wales, and for the Revolution; that wished well to the present war, and to the alliance against France, were represented as secret favourers of presbytery, and as ill affected to the church, and were called *Low Churchmen*. It was said, that they were in the church only while the law and preferments were on its side, but that they were ready to give it up as soon as they saw a proper time for declaring themselves. With these false and invidious characters did the High party endeavour to load all those who could not be brought into their measures and designs.

Own Time, v, 67-71

2 A High Church Martyr, 1705

(i) The Rev. Samuel Wesley to Bishop Wake of Lincoln, Lincoln Castle, 4 October 1705

Your Lordship knows the books I wrote concerning the dissenters... I was told when last at London... that I must retract or palliate in print what I had written on those subjects, which the dissenters had assured him were falsehoods and scandals, and that without this they would make such a clamour, and had so strong an interest, that scarce any body could serve me, and this he several times pressed me to very warmly, tho' I had often assured him there was nothing but truth in what I had published. This, and what he added, concerning the numerous friends which the dissenters expected in the next Parliament, and that all those who had affronted 'em must expect to be called to account when they came to sit, had a contrary effect to what was designed. Tho' I was poor, I could see no reason why I should be treated like a rogue and turned into an Irish evidence. I saw the growing power and insolence of the dissenters and their party, and that the Church, the clergy and the universities were every day insulted in their writings, wherein they vented the same principles I had charged 'em with, and which I knew they generally held while I lived amongst 'em. This made me think myself obliged, as well in common prudence as common honesty, to give my vote and use what little interest I had, against the election for our county, for the two old members, who could not be suspected of partiality for the dissenters; for none who was in his right senses would except against those very men in his jury who, he was morally assured, would never be biassed unjustly to bring him in guilty. Yet before I would be anything in this affair, I was so nice as to write to one of the new candidates, there having been some intimacy between us, giving him the reasons which I thought obliged me to vote against him. His friends, the dissenters and their adherents, reported there was treason in the letter, the person to whom it was sent having exposed it wherever he came for a week together; [up]on which, and not before, I gave copies which my friends told me I was obliged to do in my own vindication. Before I had done this, the other party threatened to send up my letter with such a recommendation as should do my business, and turn me out of the regiment which the Duke of Marlborough had given me, and that after this they'd throw me into gaol; and have, I thank 'em, been full as good as their words in both. They disturbed me and another clergyman in the church at divine service, proclaimed me, by name, rogue and rascal, at the head of the mob, tho' I never affronted 'em, as I never shunned 'em; shouted, huzzaed, drummed and fired guns and pistols night and day under my windows, where my wife was newly laid in childbed (of our sixteenth child); called to my children in the yard – 'you devils! we'll come and turn you all out o' doors a-begging shortly!' (what had those lambs done?); reported I was distracted (where then was their mercy?), and worse, that I preached treason, whereas I have never so much as in thought offended my gracious sovereign, and my sermons both before these troubles and in the midst of 'em will sufficiently prove my loyalty. For the finishing stroke, they threw me into gaol here for a debt to a relation of that person to whom I wrote the letter, which they might easily do, when they had sunk what little credit my many misfortunes had left me, by taking away my regiment.

Christ Church Library, Oxford, Wake MSS.
Letters I, fo. 15

(ii) Robert Harley to the Duke of Marlborough, 13 July 1705

I hear from Mr Cardonnel that your Grace has not had an account of the Queen's reasons for removing Mr Wesley from being a chaplain to the army. As far as I understand it has been upon account of his behaviour. He made it his business to speak very disrespectfully of the Queen personally, and of her Government. He pretended to discover that the Church was in great danger under the Queen's government, and he thought it necessary to propagate this doughty doctrine before the late elections in Lincolnshire.

Blenheim MSS. A.1-25

3 'A Dialogue betwixt a Bishop and a Priest', 1705

THE ARGUMENT

The Bishop of Durham, with a numerous train of ladies and gentlemen in his company, came last week to Daventry and stayed one night at the

Sheaf there. The vicar of Badby, who had lately published a book, thought it a proper time to attend his Lordship and present him with a copy of it. His design was not so much to do honour to the episcopal order, as to extort a guinea for the compliment of his present: and he had certainly compassed his end, had he in wisdom held his peace, and not rudely affronted his Lordship by his talk. But as it proved in the event, he effectually defeated his main purpose by the impudence of his discourse. And the dialogue that passed between these two in the interview may prove entertaining to a third person. 'Tis true, I have the account only by report, and by scraps, and it has been my business to put it into due form and method, and make the order seem natural. And you may depend upon it that the substance of the relation is true in every part...

B[isho]p. Mr. Edwards, your town of Badby is in the neighbourhood of Fauesly. Pray, how does my cousin Knightley do?

Ed[wards]. Truly, my Lord, I have little or no conversation with that gentleman. I waited upon him one day at his house, and was not received so civilly as to encourage me to make a second visit.

Bp. How so, Sir? My cousin Knightley is a gentleman of great civility to all men, and especially has a regard to clergymen of worth, and pays them double respect. What have you done, to induce him to go out of his usual road, and forgo his civilities to you?

Ed. I believe, my Lord, it was because we two are of different principles with respect to the government, and in the late election did not vote the same way.

Bp. Why, did you not vote for the present members? They are gentlemen of unblemished virtue and honour, and true friends to the established Church.

Ed. No my Lord I did not: I was for voting for such men as, I was sure, would please the Queen: and not for those that would endeavour to bring in the P[rince] of Wales.

Here my Lord rose with indignation from the table, and my Lady Crewe reassumed the discourse...

[When] the Bishop returned to the table... 'Here's a book (says he) in my hand, whose title-page pretends is written in defence of diocesan episcopacy: But I'll not believe an author to be in earnest with his argument whose practice is diametrically opposite to it, and tends to the subversion of diocesan episcopacy. For it is plain he contributes his utmost power to abolish the hierarchy, and introduce presbytery by his constant voting and siding with fanatics. Sir, I shall not read your treatise, and so farewell.

Exit Edwards *sine promis*.

Add. MSS. 27440, fos. 76-7

4 High Church Clergy and a Low Church Bishop, 1706

The Diary of Thomas Naish, 10 July 1706

The Bishop of Sarum, having offered an address to his clergy to be signed by them in order to be presented to the Queen upon the late glorious successes in the Netherlands and Spain, he inserted these words, *None but the confederates of our enemies, and those who are deluded by them can imagine our Church to be in danger*. The clergy for the most part were shocked at this expression, and many of them refused to sign it, for which he abused them, calling them enemies to the Queen, and factious. To wipe off this aspersion, it was thought advisable for the clergy to make a separate address, but that not appearing feasible, we petitioned the Grand Jury, that we might be admitted to the honour of joining with them in their address, which thing was granted. Whereupon I drew up the following address, which was allowed of by the Grand Jury, and after they had signed it they entrusted me with it to get as many clergymen's hands to it as I could. I went to most parts of the county with it and got the following gentlemen and clergy's hands to it,[1] and after that, 27 July, I carried it to London and gave it to my Lord Pembroke, desiring him to present it to the Queen for us, having a recommendation to him from Mr. Hyde [Tory M.P. for Wiltshire] who was foreman of the Grand Jury. His lordship accepted it, and promised me to present it in as decent a manner as he could, which he accordingly did the 29th of July. The Queen received it graciously, and his lordship

[1] Naish's Diary has been edited by Doreen Slatter and published by the *Wiltshire Archaeological and Natural History Society Records Branch*, volume xx (Devizes, 1965). The Address appears on pp. 55-6, and the names of 18 of the Grand Jury, 45 'Justices of the peace and Gentlemen' and 89 clergy are added, pp. 56-7.

desired Sir Charles Hedges [Secretary of State] to take minutes of it and to insert notice of its being presented in the *Gazette*, which was done Aug. 2nd.

Bodleian Library, MS. Top. Wilts c. 7 fo. 25

5 Party Patronage in Norfolk, 1706

Sir Charles Turner, M.P., to Robert Walpole, Kirby, 23 September 1706

Mr. Crispe, a notorious Jacobite parson in my neighbourhood of Kirby, is a-dying if not dead. His livings are St. John's, Ilketshall, in Suffolk, which is in the Lord Keeper's gift, and Ellingham in Norfolk which is Lord Walden's. This is the first opportunity I have had towards enabling myself to be a checkmate to my loving friend and neighbour Sir Edmund Bacon. There are ten or twelve freeholders in Ellingham, and as it joins to Kirby so as to be almost the same town, ... could I but get an honest parson in, I should not much question but with his assistance to strike a good stroke towards bringing those poor deluded people to their senses again.

Cholmondeley (Houghton) MSS. 534

6 Pulpit Electioneering in Durham, 1708

James Clavering to Lady Cowper, Durham, 11 May 1708

By the order of the Bishop and Chapter, as supposed, the School master ... preached before them at the Cathedral in the morning, and the same sermon in the afternoon to the Mayor and Aldermen at the market place church. The text was the verse [*sic*] of the 12th chapter of the 1st of Samuel, and the words, they say, by hard straining he perverted into the management of elections, on which his whole discourse run, lashing all those who opposed Mr Conyers, concluding that damnation would be their future lot, if they did not repent of such an heinous sin as the attempting to reject so true and trusty a member of the Church.

E. Hughes (ed.), 'Some Clavering Correspondence', *Archaeologia Aeliana*, 4th series (1956), xxxiv, 17

THE PROFESSIONS: THE ARMED FORCES AND THE LAW

The Church was not alone among the professions in experiencing the caustic, divisive effects of party conflict. The armed forces, swollen by two great wars to proportions hitherto unimagined, were inexorably drawn into the spoils system; and so, in some measure, was the legal profession. This is not to say that talent was never, or only rarely, a prime factor in professional promotion. Lord Orford of the Junto, for instance, when First Lord of the Admiralty, had 'one merit really very great and unquestionable, to have always preferred the best officers in the service'.[1] To climb the ladder quickly, however, even the talented needed influential patronage; and patronage in the years 1694-1716, whether personal or official, was a party asset and was normally expected to be exploited in a party interest.

There was already by the late seventeenth century a natural Whig bias in the lay professions. But this was increased, in the years up to 1710 at least, by the deployment of patronage. The two brightest ornaments in the legal profession between 1694 and 1716, Somers and Cowper, were both leading figures in the Whig party. It was natural that aspiring young barristers should have been attracted by their political as well as their professional example; and the fact that between them Somers and Cowper held the Great Seal of England for 14 of those 23 years gave them ample opportunity to reward their devotees. Many of those who benefited from their august patronage were able to pay off their debt by zealous service in the party cause – not merely in the House of Commons but also in the courts, where prosecutions inspired by party malice were not infrequent. One such beneficiary was Sir Thomas Parker, who as a Lord Chief Justice after March 1710 gave much succour to the Whigs in their years of persecution at the end of Anne's reign (4).

In the army the fount of all patronage from March 1702 until early in

---

[1] *The Private Correspondence of the Duchess of Marlborough* (1838), i, 194: Arthur Mainwaring to the Duchess, n.d. [1709].

I THE PROFESSIONS: THE ARMED FORCES AND THE LAW 59

1710 was the Captain-General, Marlborough. By the middle years of Anne Tory military men had become firmly convinced that the duke was using this great power largely in the interests of their political opponents, whose party had consistently shown more enthusiasm in Parliament for the large-scale land campaigns in the Low Countries which Marlborough himself favoured. These charges did no justice to Marlborough's sense of responsibility and professional judgement; but there was a degree of substance in them, and they were given point by the spectacular rise to general's rank after 1702 of particular favourites of the Captain-General, like Cadogan, Palmes, Meredith and the rake-hell Macartney – all of them fierce Whigs, and three of them members of Parliament. Moreover, having Marlborough's ear, the Whig generals were able to use their influence to affect promotion prospects at regimental level also (1). Once Robert Harley had replaced Godolphin at the Treasury there was a swift reaction against the Whig supremacy in the army. A number of major appointments in the summer and autumn of 1710 were made, over Marlborough's head, in favour of Tory officers, and three of the most notable Churchill *protégés* were ignominiously stripped of their commands and forced out of the profession for political indiscretions (2, 3). Long before the Captain-General's dismissal in December 1711 his wings had been effectively clipped.

The most blatant interference with the army for party ends, however, was still to come. In 1713-14 there was a Tory attempt, inspired by Lord Bolingbroke, to work officers of Jacobite sympathies into key military positions, an attempt that was only nipped in the bud by Anne's sudden death. After August 1714, with Marlborough restored to supreme command, the war over and the prospect of civil disturbance ahead, it seemed essential to the victorious party that the army should at last be made safe for Whiggery. By contrast, the purge of the judiciary after George I's accession was less dramatic, thanks in part to the admirable restraint of Lord Chancellor Cowper. But even in this field the change of ruler gave the Whigs the opportunity to weed out a number of their most prominent opponents from the bench of Common Law judges,[1] and to reward many of their own parliamentary champions, such as Lechmere, King and Pratt, with judicial plums (5).

---

[1] It was a post-Revolution convention, embodied in statute law after 1714, that English judges were not removable, during good behaviour, until the death of the sovereign who had appointed them.

1 Politics, Patronage and Promotion in the Camp, 1705

Letters of Major J. Cranstoun to Robert Cunningham:

Camp at Herenthals, 1 October 1705

Most of our army here are Whigs, and staunch ones, and so are very glad to hear that the Court have now for the first time declared themselves so much above-board as that of the Lord Treasurer's recommending Mr. Smith for Speaker seems to be. If this is sincere things must go well in the ensuing session.

We have not here made any progress in the war this campaign answerable to our own and our friends' expectations of us. Faults there have been and miscarriages, and those great too, but where to lodge them is hard to tell, and we hope you will not look too narrowly into them since it cannot probably do any good. It is certain that when our army was on the Moselle Prince Louis and the Germans disappointed us much; ... but people who are ill-natured pretend to censure in [the Duke of Marlborough] the project of going there with an army of 80 or 90,000 men to lie seven or eight weeks – which he must have done to have taken Saarlouis and Metz – in a country where the French, who have been long masters of it, say they could never subsist 25 or 30,000 men six weeks ... This is what the ill-natured people amongst us and such as envy the Duke of Marlborough's glory say of the first part of our campaign; nobody denies but the Duke came in season to relieve the States, who were trembling for their towns, but they say they neither sought nor expected that he should have brought back his whole army to them or abandoned absolutely the designs laid on the Moselle ...

[The Dutch] and others also complain a little that the Duke does not advise so much either with the officers of experience and in the highest characters of his own and the States army as with two or three favourites whom he himself has raised, such as Brigadier Cadogan, Brigadier Palmes and Brigadier Meredith, who are men of little service and experience. It is certain our army is now very weak, and we have lost this summer in the British troops almost as many men by marauding and desertion, though we have not fought at all, as we lost last summer though we had two bloody battles.

I POLITICS, PATRONAGE AND PROMOTION IN THE CAMP 61

Camp at Calemthout, 20 October 1705

The subject of this is to acquaint you that Brigadier Ferguson died at the Bosch on the 12th instant of a high malignant fever ... Our regiment has a great loss, and I in particular more than they all, for he allowed me all his confidence and all his friendship. Many have already put in for our regiment, as Lord Mark Kerr, Lord Edward Murray, but principally Colonel Macartney, who having but a new-raised regiment, which must probably be broke at the peace, he seeks to obtain ours, and has found the way to get Brigadiers Cadogan, Meredith and Palmes to recommend him, and they you know are looked on with us as the three great favourites with the Duke. Lieutenant Colonel Borthwick, who is our Lieutenant Colonel, is allowed by all indifferent people to have the only just right to it. He is an honest, plain, brave man, and a good officer ... [and] by his rank and the course of his service as well as by his merit and bravery, ought to have the regiment in justice. If he gets it, my preferment to be Lieutenant Colonel ought and I hope will follow in the same course; but if any other Colonel is brought over his head it stops of consequence both my advancement and all the officers in course below me ...

The Duke seems at least as favourable to Colonel Borthwick as to any of his rivals, ... and told him that he knew the particular circumstances and constitution of our regiment very well, would have a tender regard to it, and assured him the regiment should not be disposed of till he were satisfied. But this we fear may be a design to give Colonel Macartney our regiment and give Borthwick his, which is what I know the favourites all solicit ... Our whole officers and soldiers have such a terror of Colonel Macartney's coming upon our head that they are all in despair about it, looking upon the regiment as inevitably ruined; for he who has already squandered all his own and lady's fortune, and I fear her children's also, and has in one year by his gaming and rioting run his own regiment in debt ... must by these measures not only oppress but soon utterly ruin any regiment he gets.

Hist. MSS. Comm. *Portland MSS.* iv, 250-1, 255, 265-6

2 The Harley Ministry and the Army, 1710

Besides the ... changes in the civil employments, it was thought necessary, in order to strengthen the hands of the new ministry and the Church party, to do justice to some military gentlemen who seemed to have been neglected under the last ministry. Upon this consideration the earl of Portmore, a brave and experienced general, who had distinguished himself on many occasions in the late war (under the name of Sir David Collier) and whose involuntary idleness was lamented by all the well-wishers to the common cause, was appointed commander in chief of her Majesty's forces in Portugal, in the room of the earl of Galway, whose advanced age and infirmities rendered him unfit for action, not to mention his intimacy with the late Treasurer.

On the other hand, the Lord Windsor, who some years before had a fine regiment of horse taken from him (either for not voting in the House of Commons according to the desire of the Great Man beforementioned, or for opposing the election of his son, the Lord Rialton [at Cambridge in 1705]) was now restored to her Majesty's favour, and advanced to the post of a Lieutenant-General. At the same time General Webb, to whose memorable victory at Wynendale the allies were principally indebted for the conquest of the important town of Lisle, but whose glory was at first like to have been given to one that had no share in that action,[1] was appointed Governor of the Isle of Wight.

A. Boyer, *The Political State of Great Britain*, i, 8

3 The Disgrace of Three Whig Generals, December 1710

(i) Henry St. John to John Drummond, 12 December 1710

The Queen has thought fit to dismiss Mr. Meredyth, Mr. MacKartney and Mr. Honeywood from her service; and the reason which she commands her servants to give for this step is that she found it absolutely necessary to stop the licentious insolence which was used the last campaign, both towards her and towards her administration, by these examples; that she hopes these will suffice, and that she shall not be obliged to make any more.

Letters of revocation go by this post to Mr. Cadogan, and your friend, Mr. Hill, is already appointed her Majesty's envoy-extraordinary and plenipotentiary to the States and at Brussels.

Letters and Correspondence of Henry St. John, Lord Viscount Bolingbroke (ed. G. Parke, 1798), i, 38-9

[1] Viz. Marlborough's favourite, Cadogan, who at first received the credit for this victory in the *Gazette*.

3 THE DISGRACE OF THREE WHIG GENERALS, 1710

(ii) [London, 13 December 1710]

You hear the havoc making in the army. Meredyth, Macartney and colonel Honeywood are obliged to sell their commands at half value, and leave the army, for drinking destruction to the present ministry, and dressing up a hat on a stick and calling it Harley; then drinking a glass with one hand, and discharging a pistol with the other at the maukin, wishing it were Harley himself, and a hundred other such pretty tricks, as inflaming their soldiers and foreign ministers against the late changes at Court. Cadogan has had a little paring; his mother told me yesterday he had lost the place of envoy: but I hope they will go no further with him, for he was not at those mutinous meetings.

Jonathan Swift, *Journal to Stella*

4 Lord Chief Justice Parker and the Parties at Derby, September 1710

We have an account from Derby that the [Whig] faction there and in those parts are so enraged at the dissolution of the Parliament and the change that the Queen has made in her ministry that they care not what they say or do. They declare the Queen has no hereditary right, and that all the right she has to govern is given her by virtue of an Act of Parliament made by her own subjects, and that they have reason to believe that there is a P[rince] of W[ales] in being who was lawfully begotten and whose health they often drink on their bare knees.[1]

Some of these were to have been prosecuted at the Sessions holden at Derby on the 25th past. But care was taken by a person in an eminent post, who is also the R[ecorder] there,[2] to prevent the design by adding 15 rank Whigs to an honest Grand Jury that had been empanelled some time before, in order to have found the bills *ignoramus*; and on the other hand, to discourage the Churchmen several persons were ordered to be indicted for a riot for crying about the streets the names of the loyal candidates that are designed to represent that city. This with several other hardships that are put upon the Church party there they complain of.

Brit. Mus. Loan 29/321: Dyer's Newsletter
3 October 1710

[1] Dyer's flagrant Tory bias makes his evidence on this point, to say the least, dubious.
[2] The Lord Chief Justice, Sir Thomas Parker, was the Recorder of Derby and had been a Whig member for the borough from 1705 until March 1710.

5 Lord Cowper's Advice to George I on Judicial Appointments, 1714

JUDGES

King's Bench

Lord Chief Justice Parker
Sir Littleton Powis
Mr. Justice Eyre[s]
Sir Thomas Powis

This Court has the great influence on corporations. The 2 brothers generally act, in those matters, in opposition to the Chief Justice and Mr. Justice Eyres[1]: therefore it would be of great use if one of their places was supplied by another fit man.

Sir Littleton, the elder brother, is a man of less abilities and consequence, but blameless. Sir Thomas of better abilities, but more culpable; having been Attorney General to the late King James to his abdication, and zealously instrumental in most of the steps which ruined that prince and brought those great dangers on the kingdom. Besides having from that time practised the law with great profit, he lately, when the hopes of the Pretender's party were raised, laid down his practice of near £4000 a year to be a judge, not worth £1500 a year, for no visible reason; but if the Pretender had succeeded he would have made, and that very justly, a merit of this step.

If either of these be removed, I humbly recommend Serjeant Pratt,[2] who the Chief Justice, Mr. Justice Eyres and I believe every one that knows him will approve.

Common Pleas

Lord Chief Justice Trevor
Mr. Justice Blencow
Mr. Justice Tracey
Mr. Justice Dormer

There seems to be no objection to the three last. The first is an able man, but made one of the twelve lords which the late ministry procured to be created at once (in such haste that few, if any, of their patents had any preamble or reasons of their creation), only to support *their Peace*,

[1] Robert Eyres, Solicitor-General in the Whig administration of 1708-10.
[2] John Pratt, Whig M.P. for Midhurst, 1711-14.

which the House of Lords, they found, would not without that addition. From that time, at least, he went violently into all the measures of that ministry, and was much trusted by them; and when they divided a little before the Queen's death, he sided with Lord Bolingbroke, and for so doing, 'tis credibly said, was to have been made Lord President. Many of the Lords think his being a peer an objection to his being a judge ... and tis said that the suitors dislike the difference they find in his behaviour to them since he had this distinction. He is grown very wealthy. If it be thought fit to remove him, Sir Peter King, Recorder of the City of London,[1] I should humbly propose as fit to succeed him.

> Exchequer
>
> Lord Chief Baron – vacant
> Baron Berry
> Baron Price
> Baron Smith, Chief Baron of the Exchequer in Scotland also
> Baron Banister

The general opinion of Westminster Hall is that Mr. Dodd, an ancient practiser of this Court, is the fittest person to supply the place of Chief Baron, now void, and I must confess experience is requisite for this post above all others. Lord Halifax recommends his brother, Sir James Montagu, who has been Attorney General to the late Queen; and my partiality to gratify my Lord's desires would incline me to wish he may succeed. But if Mr. Dodd be thought more proper, perhaps Sir James Montagu would be pretty well content to be a Baron, at least for the present; which might be effected by removing Baron Banister, a man not at all qualified for his place (which he owes to the friendship of the late Chancellor [the Tory, Lord Harcourt]), as any lord will inform your Majesty ...

Of your Majesty's Council learned in the law, I beg leave to mention at this time only the

> Attorney General, and
> Solicitor General.

They who are at present in your Majesty's service generally incline to remove both, and put in their places Sir Peter King, above mentioned,

---

[1] Whig M.P. for Beeralston, 1701-14.

and Mr. Lechmere. But they are so near rivals they will never agree the one to act under the other in those stations; which is another reason why Sir Peter may be more fitly disposed of as above said, in the Common Pleas.

The Attorney General, Sir Edward Northey, is an excellent lawyer and a man of great abilities in the law, a moderate Tory, and much respected by that party, and no further blameable than by obeying those who could command him if he kept his place. If he should not be removed, 'tis reasonable to think Mr. Lechmere would accept of being Solicitor under him, he being old and infirm, and there being no competition between them as to seniority or pre-eminence in their profession.

Lord Campbell, *Lives of the Lord Chancellors*, iv, 349-50

J

THE PRESS

For politics as for journalism, the end of Stuart censorship of the press, with the lapsing of the Licensing Act in 1695, proved a seminal event. To it can be directly traced the spectacular rise of 'Grub Street', that fictitious abode of a new generation of political writers whose many different talents – whether for exposition, demolition, satire or mere abuse – were recruited by the Whig and Tory parties.

The most important effect in the long run of the end of censorship was the stimulus it gave to the propagation of the newspaper. A divided society required a more varied news service than could be provided by the official *Gazette*. In response to this need there emerged the privately edited sheet or half-sheet, appearing normally thrice weekly, which combined a high proportion of fairly standardised foreign news and advertising space with a small but often telling element of domestic comment. The popularity of the newspapers was an important factor in inducing the Commons in 1698 to throw out a bill designed to reimpose a form of censorship; and it is significant that by this time debate inside and outside the House was genuinely concerned with the freedom of the press (**2**), which had by no means been the central issue in 1695.[1]

By 1709 almost a score of newspapers were appearing in London alone, and most of them were politically committed, like Abel Roper's *Post Boy* which supported the Tories, or George Ridpath's *Flying-Post* which was equally firm to the Whigs. The reporting of parliamentary debates was still a breach of privilege (**1**); but one field which did give scope to the partisan editor was the coverage of General Elections. After 1708, especially, this grew increasingly ambitious. Instead of confining themselves in the main to publishing lists of successful candidates, papers began to print party manifestos, many polls, and a selection of reports from various constituencies (**3**).

Frequent elections, an abundance of controversial issues and an eager public made this a golden age for the political pamphleteer. In the hands of skilful practitioners like Defoe, Mainwaring, Clement, Swift or Atterbury the pamphlet could become a best-seller. Scurrility, and boldness in attacking those in authority were, as always, good selling points in any publication, and the leading politicians of the period needed to develop elephantine skins to withstand the barbs of 'the scribblers'. Some never succeeded in doing so (**5**).

Virulent party propaganda was far from being the preserve of professional journalists: learned divines like Francis Atterbury and White Kennett and busy politicians like Robert Walpole also learned to exploit the new freedom of the press with devastating skill. The reverend Dr. Jonathan Swift not only surpassed all his contemporaries in the art of pamphleteering but pioneered the sophisticated political weekly. His early numbers of *The Examiner* were masterpieces of journalistic satire for his Tory readers to savour in coffee-house, club or vicarage (**4**).

While the party men on the whole revelled in their new media, the government became seriously alarmed. Its first reaction was to look for ways and means of putting its own case in contradistinction to that of the two warring parties (**6, i**), and Daniel Defoe's *Review* proved for some years an effective solution to this problem. Subsequently official thinking became more concerned with stemming the flood from the printing presses, and this negative approach eventually produced the stamp duty of 1712, which many writers gloomily forecast would bring about the death of Grub Street (**6, ii**). They were wrong. The press certainly suffered a severe mauling in the first years of the new

[1] Most of the pressure to end the licensing system in 1695 had come from opponents of the special privileges of the Stationers' Company.

duty[1]; but while some editors and printers went under, many others survived to carry the tradition of a vigorous political journalism into the age of Walpole. For one thing, the pamphlet remained a most effective weapon; indeed Richard Steele's *The Crisis* provoked a leading member of the Oxford ministry to protest to the Commons in March 1714 that 'unless means are found to restrain the licentiousness of the Press, and to shelter those who have the honour to be in the administration from malicious and scandalous libels, they who by their abilities are best qualified to serve their Queen and Country will decline public offices and employments'. Furthermore, the future of the political journal, combining literary with partisan appeal, was never in serious jeopardy. The success in 1713-14 of *The Englishman*, whose insinuations of Jacobitism against the ministry brought down the wrath of the House of Commons upon its author's head (**6, iii**), emphasised the limitations of the stamp duty so long as there was an avid readership prepared to pay for true quality.

1 Illicit Reporting of Parliamentary Debates, 1694

[21 December 1694]

A complaint being made to this House that * Dyer, a News Letter writer, has presumed in his News Letter to take notice of the proceedings of this House;

Resolved, that the said * Dyer be summoned by the Serjeant at Arms to attend this House tomorrow morning at ten a clock, to answer the said complaint.

[22 December 1694]

The House being informed that * Dyer, the News Letter writer, attended according to the order of yesterday, he was called in, and heard touching the complaint made against him: and, acknowledging the offence, humbly begged the pardon of the House for the same. And then withdrew.

Ordered, that the said * Dyer be brought to the Bar and, upon his

---

[1] See J. M. Price, 'A Note on the Circulation of the London Press', *Bulletin of the Institute of Historical Research* (1958) xxxi, 215-24.

knees, reprimanded by Mr. Speaker for his great presumption. And accordingly he was brought in and reprimanded.

Ordered, that the said * Dyer be discharged, paying his fees.

Resolved, that no News Letter writers do, in their letters or other papers that they disperse, presume to intermeddle with the debates or any other proceedings of this House.

Commons' Journals, xi, 192-3

2 The Case for a Free Press, 1697

A Letter to a Member of Parliament, showing that a restraint on the Press is inconsistent with the Protestant religion, and dangerous to the liberties of the nation (1697)

Sir, according to your commands, I here present you with those reasons that oblige me to oppose the restraining of the Press, as inconsistent with the Protestant religion and dangerous to the liberties of the nation: both which I undertake to show. And in order to prove the first, I beg leave to premise, first, that which makes a man to differ from a brute, wholly uncapable of forming any notion of religion, is his reason; which is the only light God has given him, not only to discover that there is a religion but to distinguish the true from the many false ones ... Now the way that a man's reason does this is by examining those proofs, arguments or mediums that either himself or others have found out, and by comparing them with his common and self-evident notions, by means of which he finds out the agreement or disagreement of any proposition with those standards and tests of truth ... It is men's mutual duty to inform each other in those propositions they apprehend to be true, and the arguments by which they endeavour to prove them: which cannot be done so well as by printing them, ten thousand books, after the letters are once set, being sooner printed than one transcribed ...

The greatest enjoyment that rational and sociable creatures are capable of is to employ their thoughts on what subject they please, and to communicate them to one another as freely as they think them; and herein consists the dignity and freedom of human nature, without which no other liberty can be secure. For what is it that enables a few tyrants to keep almost all mankind in slavery but their narrow and wrong notions of government? which is owing to the discouragement they lie under of mutually communicating, and consequently of employing, their thoughts on political matters... The arts of state, in most countries, being to enslave the people or to keep them in slavery, it became a crime to talk, much more to write, about political matters: and ever since printing has been invented, there have been in most places state-licensers, to hinder men from freely writing about government; for which there can be no other reason but to prevent the defects of either the government or the management of it from being discovered and amended... In a word, all sorts of men whose interest is not to have their actions exposed to the public, which I am afraid are no small number, will be for restraining the Press, and perhaps will add iniquity to iniquity by pretending they do it out of conscience to suppress immorality and profaneness.

But this is not the worst that may happen; because the Press may be so managed as to become a most powerful engine to overturn and subvert the very constitution. For should a magistrate arise with arbitrary designs in his head, no papers that plead the rights and just privileges of the people would be stamped with an *imprimatur*. Then the Press would be employed only to extend the prerogative beyond all bounds, and to extol the promoters of arbitrary power as the chief patriots of their country, and to expose and traduce those that were really so...

I might add a great number of other reasons, because as many things as are worth knowing, so many arguments there are for the liberty of the Press... I shall only say that for my own part I should be glad, especially when at a distance from London (and I suppose other country gentlemen may be of the same mind) to divert myself with some other newspapers besides the Gazette, which would hardly be permitted if the Press were regulated.

Printed in *Parl. Hist.* v, App. xiii, pp. cxxx-i, cxlv-vi, cxlviii-ix

3 A Newspaper Election Report, 1710

On Friday... came on the election for the borough of Pembroke. Sir Arthur Owen and Lewis Wogan, esquire, were candidates. Sir Arthur Owen had 283 voices and Lewis Wogan, esquire, 335. But the Mayor, being a dissenter and the son of a Presbyterian preacher, does declare that he will return Sir Arthur Owen.

Haverfordwest, October 17th. The election for the county of Pembroke came on this day. The candidates were Sir Arthur Owen, bart., and John Barlow, esquire. Sir Arthur polled his votes, in all 190. Mr. Barlow polled till night came on, and then, being unwilling to detain the gentlemen, dismissed them, well satisfied with the defeat he had given the enemy, without the help of the body of reserve, polling only 493. In this election the diligence of the clergy was remarkable, 50 of them polling for Mr. Barlow. But there was a Judas among the apostles; 7 of them polled for Sir Arthur . . .

Coventry, October 20th . . . Robert Craven (brother to the Right Honourable the Lord Craven) and Thomas Gery, esquires, were, upon a vast majority . . . declared duly elected by two sheriffs chosen on purpose to serve the Whig interest . . . The issue of this election is the more remarkable because the government of this corporation is in the hands of professed dissenters, who have of late been notorious for electing persons of known disaffection to, and activity against, the Church; and [who] made choice of these officers with a desire to procure the return of their old members, and it's thought at the instigation of a gentleman [Lord Sunderland, Recorder of Coventry] lately gone for London. It's further observable that Sir W[illiam] Boughton, Sir Richard Newdigate, William Bromley Esq., and a great number of persons of distinction, and clergymen, appeared in favour of the Church candidates; whereas the other party was made up of mean tradesmen and the scum of the rabble. The night ended with ringing of bells, illuminations, bonfires and all other demonstrations of a public satisfaction.

The Post Boy, No. 2411, 24-26 October 1710

4 Swift on the Resurrection of the Whigs, 1711

. . . But to come to the subject I have now undertaken, which is to examine what the consequences would be upon the supposition that the Whigs were now restored to their power. I already imagine the present free Parliament dissolved, and another of a different epithet met, by the force of money and management. I read immediately a dozen or two of stinging votes against the proceedings of the late ministry. The bill now to be repealed [the General Naturalization Act] would then be re-enacted, and the birthright of an Englishman reduced again to the value of twelvepence. But to give the reader a strong imagination of such a scene, let me represent the designs of some men, lately endeavoured and projected, in the form of a paper of votes.

Ordered, that a bill be brought in for repealing the sacramental test.

A petition of Tindal, Collins, Clendon, Coward and Toland, in behalf of themselves and many hundreds of their disciples, some of whom are members of this honourable house, desiring that leave may be given to bring in a bill for qualifying atheists, deists and Socinians to serve their country in any employment, ecclesiastical, civil or military.

Ordered, that leave be given to bring in a bill according to the prayer of the said petition; and that Mr. Lechmere do prepare and bring in the same.

Ordered, that a bill be brought in for removing the education of youth out of the hands of the clergy . . .

Another for constituting a general for life; with instructions to the committee that care may be taken to make the war last as long as the life of the said general.

A bill of attainder against Charles duke of Shrewsbury, John duke of Buckingham, Laurence earl of Rochester, Sir Simon Harcourt, knight, Robert Harley and William Shippen, esqrs., Abigail Masham, spinster, and others, for high treason against the junto.

Resolved, that Sarah, duchess of Marlborough, has been a most dutiful, just and grateful servant to her Majesty.

Resolved, that to advise the dissolution of a Whig Parliament or the removal of a Whig ministry was in order to bring in Popery and the Pretender; and that the said advice was high treason.

Resolved, that by the original compact the government of this realm is by a junto, and king or queen; but the administration solely in the junto . . .

Ordered, that it be a standing order of this House that the merit of elections be not determined by the number of voices, or right of electors, but by weight; and that one Whig shall weigh down ten Tories . . .

These and the like reformations would, in all probability, be the first fruits of the Whigs' resurrection; and what structures such able artists might in a short time build upon such foundations I leave others to conjecture.

The Examiner, No. 26, 25 Jan. 1711

5 The Politicians and the Press

(i) [Robert Harley], Earl of Oxford to the Duke of Marlborough, 19 October 1711

As to the contents of your Grace's letter of the 19th [N.S.], I hope my sentiments are so fully known of that villainous way of libelling, I need say little to your Grace upon that subject. When I had the honour to be Secretary of State I did, by an impartial prosecution, silence most of them, until a party of men [the Whigs], for their own ends, supported them against the laws and my prosecution. I do assure your Grace I abhor the practice as mean and disingenuous. I have made it so familiar to myself, by some years' experience, that as I know I am every week, if not every day, in some libel or other, so I would willingly compound that all the ill-natured scribblers should have licence to write ten times more against me, upon condition they would write against nobody else. I do assure your Grace I neither know nor desire to know any of the authors; and, as I heartily wish this barbarous war was at an end, I shall be very ready to take my part in suppressing them.

W. Coxe, *Memoirs of the Duke of Marlborough* (Bohn, 1848), iii, 261

(ii) Swift and Nottingham, December 1711

[5 December]

Lord Nottingham, a famous Tory and speechmaker, is gone over to the Whig side. They toast him daily, and Lord Wharton says, 'It is Dismal (so they call him from his looks) will save England at last'. Lord Treasurer [Oxford] was hinting as if he wished a ballad was made on him, and I will get up one against tomorrow. He gave me a scurrilous printed paper of bad verses on himself, under the name of the English Catiline, and made me read them to the company ...

[6 December]

I was this morning making the ballad, two degrees above Grub Street; at noon I paid a visit to Mrs. Masham, and then went to dine with our society... We were eleven met, the greatest meeting we ever had. I am next week to introduce Lord Orrery. The printer came before we parted and brought the ballad, which made them laugh very heartily a dozen times...

[18 December]

There was printed a Grub Street speech of Lord Nottingham; and he was such an owl to complain of it in the House of Lords, who have taken up the printer for it. I heard at Court that Walpole (a great Whig member) said that I and my whimsical club writ it at one of our meetings, and that I should pay for it. He will find he lies: and I shall let him know by a third hand my thoughts of him.

Journal to Stella

6 The Government, the Commons and the Press

(i) Robert Harley to Lord Godolphin, Brampton, 9 August 1702

... I had not troubled your Lordship with the idle story of the quarrel in this country but for the endeavours [which] had been used in these parts to asperse the government, which I hope is now pretty well at an end. I cannot but upon this occasion again take the liberty to offer to your Lordship that it will be of great service to have some discreet writer of the government side, if it were only to state facts right; for the generality err for want of knowledge, and being imposed upon by the stories raised by ill designing men.

Add. MSS. 28055, fo. 3

(ii) Swift on the Death of Grub Street

Do you know that Grub Street is dead and gone last week? No more ghosts or murders now for love or money. I plied it pretty close the last fortnight, and published at least seven penny papers of my own, besides some of other people's: but now every single half-sheet pays a half-penny to the Queen. The 'Observator' is fallen; the 'Medleys' are jumbled together with the 'Flying-Post'; the 'Examiner' is deadly sick; the 'Spectator' keeps up, and doubles its price; I know not how long it will hold. Have you seen the red stamp the papers are marked with: Methinks it is worth a half-penny the stamping.

* * *

These devils of Grub Street rogues that write the 'Flying-Post' and 'Medley' in one paper will not be quiet. They are always mauling Lord Treasurer, Lord Bolingbroke and me. We have the dog under prosecution, but Bolingbroke is not active enough; but I hope to swinge him. He is a Scotch rogue, one Ridpath. They get out upon bail and write on. We take them again, and [they] get fresh bail; so it goes round.
Journal to Stella, 7 August, 28 October 1712

(iii) The Expulsion of Richard Steele from the House of Commons, 1714

Baron Schütz to Baron Bothmar, London, 19 March 1714 (transl.)

Yesterday the Lower House was taken up with the accusation against Richard Steele, Esq., and I was there myself for more than three hours. Mr. Foley, who had spoken against *The Crisis* and against *The Englishman* some days before, said that he expected Mr. Steele to make it clear whether or not the marked passages in these two writings were his work, and that if they were, he must defend them. Thereupon Mr. Steele got up to say that, having compared his manuscripts with the passages which they had extracted from the above books, he recognised and avowed them as part of his work, and that he had written them in the interests of the Protestant succession in the House of Hanover, to which he was determined to remain as firm as the oaths which he had taken demanded of him; he had abjured the Pretender and he still continued to abjure him. Having said this he made a compliment to the House, to whose justice he appealed.

Mr. Walpole and Mr. Stanhope, who sat beside him, rose after him to say that having read and reread these passages, they could find nothing in them which required to be explained, or which could not be acknowledged and recognised in front of every court in England; thus, according to them, the burden of proving the evil of these writings rested with the member who had complained of them. There were many more speeches, both for and against; but on this point the Court party, which was unwilling or unable to charge Mr. Steele with anything further, demanded that he should at once proceed to make his defence. Those members who spoke for him were Lord Finch, Lord Lumley, Messrs. Pulteney and Boscawen, and several Scots, while Messrs. Bromley, Foley, Gore, Caesar, Harley and Sir William Windham declared against him. Dr. Sacheverell's name was mentioned in the debate, and those on the Court side betrayed their affection for him, but at length, having been unable to gain their point by force of argument, they called for the question. Steele's supporters were aware by then that their party was the weaker and wanted to avoid a division, but Steele was resolved to defend himself...

At this stage all strangers were obliged to leave the House; indeed the heat in the chamber had become so terrible that it was almost unbearable, and I myself withdrew at this time. Mr. Steele then began his defence, deploring the fact that, after all the trouble he had taken in composing his works to put into them nothing that was contrary to the laws of the country, nor anything that could reasonably cause offence to anyone, he was now forced to rack his brains to discover in his writings the very things which he had taken such great care not to put there. This explanation of the marked passages took him two and three quarter hours; and as the speech was so very long he read it all. When he had finished it he retired, and there began a debate which did not end until midnight... Of those who spoke in his defence the most forceful was Mr. Walpole. He spoke for an hour and a half, replying article by article, and with every sentence raking the ministry with his volleys, which were as witty as they were powerful... However, Steele's enemies, being sure of their majority, pressed for the question; and they carried it by 245 votes against 152 that the papers called *The Englishman* and *The Crisis*, written by Richard Steele, a member of the House, are scandalous and seditious, containing several expressions reflecting on the Queen, the nobility, the clergy and the universities of these Kingdoms, maliciously insinuating that the Protestant succession in the House of Hanover is in danger under her Majesty's administration, and tending to alienate the affection of all the Queen's good subjects and to sow divisions and jealousies among them. Resolved, that Richard Steele for his offence in having written and published these scandalous and seditious libels should be expelled the House.

Brit. Mus. Stowe MSS. 226, fos. 306-8

K

THE MOB

It is difficult to gauge with any accuracy the degree of political consciousness among the lower orders during the period 1694-1716. Our main criterion must necessarily be the prevalence of popular disorder, and for obvious reasons, and not least the difficulty of judging the spontaneity of many riots, it is an imperfect one. Yet it does allow us to reach two conclusions fairly confidently. One is that triennial Parliaments made the urban election mob, for twenty years at least, a serious factor in English politics. The second is that political participation by the unenfranchised masses increased markedly after 1701 and, on electoral evidence at least, reached its peak from 1710-15. Most of the more violent manifestations of popular discontent during the second half of King William's reign were plainly related to economic grievances.[1] In Anne's reign and in the opening years of George I's large sections of the working class continued to suffer periods of hardship. But the fact that in their riots they now fought each other at least as frequently as they demonstrated against revenue officials, merchants or employers, reflects the development even at this level of crude party allegiances. For the most part these allegiances seem to have been fashioned by a few simple prejudices: dislike of foreigners, fear of impressment (and therefore of a prolonged war), and above all, religious bigotry.

If the political activity of the mob was fitful this was mainly because, in the nature of things, their opportunities for self-expression were fairly limited. Major public events like coronations gave them some scope; so too did the celebration of popular anniversaries. Even the birthday of the exiled Prince of Wales in 1695 furnished the occasion for a Jacobite riot in Drury Lane (1); but on anniversaries that were publicly recognised, like the accession-day of Queen Elizabeth or, after 1702, that of William III, it was a very much easier matter for a group of ringleaders, with the aid of a few barrels of ale, to whip up anti-Papist or anti-French feeling into a rowdy demonstration (3).

---

[1] See Max Beloff, *Public Order and Popular Disturbances 1660-1714* (1938), chapters 3, 4 and 5, *passim*.

Lord Oxford and his government colleagues reacted with understandable alarm to the news in November 1711 that a massive demonstration against their peace policy was being planned to coincide with Queen Elizabeth's accession-day; for still fresh in their minds was the memory of the fierce Sacheverell riots in 1710, when dissenting meeting-houses were wrecked and the lives and limbs of prominent Whigs placed in considerable danger (2). The forces of law and order were painfully inadequate to cope with large-scale disorders until they were already well under way, and even then there was a reluctance to call in the military. Hence the need for the Riot Act in 1715.

Apart, however, from the Sacheverell trial and the '15 Rebellion, it was parliamentary elections which gave Whig and Tory mobs the best opportunities to make their presence and prejudices felt. The first General Election after the passing of the Triennial Act (1695), with disturbances in Westminster and Exeter, heralded the new era of popular disorder in the constituencies.[1] The election mobs of London and Westminster earned a special reputation for violence, but there could be equally ugly scenes in the provinces, especially when large bands of townsfolk were armed and incited by the rival party organisations, as at Coventry in 1705 and at Bristol in 1713. Both these elections were the scenes of pitched battles in the streets (4). In these and in all its political outbursts the mob was no respecter of persons. During the contest at Salisbury in 1705 the Duke of Somerset, the proudest peer in England, suffered what Defoe called 'strange insults' at the hands of a rampaging Tory mob, and John Dolben, the member of Parliament for Liskeard, who had first moved Sacheverell's impeachment, had a narrow escape from lynching during the riots of 1710 (2, i).

1 Jacobitism in Drury Lane, 1695

Tuesday, 11 June: Yesterday being the birthday of the pretended Prince of Wales, several Jacobites met in several places, and particularly at the Dog Tavern in Drury Lane, where with kettle drums, trumpets, etc, they caroused; and having a bonfire near that place, would have forced some of the spectators to have drank the said Prince's health, which they refusing occasioned a tumult. Upon which the mob gathering entered the tavern, where they did much damage and put the Jacobites to flight, some of which are taken into custody, viz.

[1] *Ibid*, p. 49.

Captain George Porter, Mr. Goodman, the late player, Mr. Bedding, Mr. Pate, etc.

> N. Luttrell, *A Brief Historical Relation of State Affairs*, iii, 483-4

2 The Sacheverell Riots, 1710

(i) Abigail Harley to Edward Harley, 2 March 1710

Last post I told you the Governor was indisposed with a great cold; indeed came that night very ill from Westminster Hall, was so ill all day yesterday was forced to keep his bed till near eight at night... About that time Sacheverell's mob pulled down Mr. Burgess's meeting-house, and burnt it in these [Lincoln's Inn] fields; did not so much as spare the poor woman's clothes that lived in the house, but burnt all she had but a feather bed. From thence they went to four more and showed the same rage. As they were gutting that in Drury Lane some horse and foot guards came and dispersed them, seized several who were committed, and several were killed in their zeal for this good cause. They attempted the same in the City, but the weavers rose, and then the train-bands, so secured all there; now we hear nothing but drums. The Fields have now several companies of the train-bands to secure the houses from the insolence of the mob. This is methinks an odd way of defending passive obedience and non-resistance. It was told me that in Oxford the same is done; till you tell me so I shall suspend my crediting that.

The mob insulted my Lord Chancellor [Cowper] and Lord Wharton last night, and caught [John] Dolben and were going to hang him upon a tree till he swore he was not Dolben, nor a Parliament man. They threatened Gil. of Sarum [Bishop Burnet] . . . I pray God it stop here.

> Hist. MSS. Comm. *Portland MSS.* iv, 532-3

(ii) Sir John Perceval to Philip Perceval, 2 March 1710

... Tomorrow we expect Sacheverell will answer to his charge, who has six lawyers to plead for him, of whom Sir Simon Harcourt is the principal. The mob grow every day more and more troublesome. They stop gentlemen's coaches and make them pull off their hats to his name. They pulled down a meeting-house at Derby, and have begun to break the windows of that where Dr. Burgess preaches, but they suspend the entire demolishing of it till they see if the Lords condemn him [Sacheverell]. They met my groom last night and asked who he was for, and he answered the Queen. Then they asked him if not for Sacheverell too, and he had the luck to answer yes, for they told him if he had said no they had knocked him down.

As the Doctor passes the streets to go to trial they hang about his coach and follow it all the way, hallowing and hooping. Higgins was in Man's Coffee House yesterday and fell out with an officer about this matter, which ended in his being shoved out of the room. But the mob came next morning and broke the windows, throwing dirt and stones into the house. Nevertheless I hope there is no danger of their interrupting the trial; for were the man ever so innocent, the legislature ought to take its course and be submitted to: otherwise every guilty man will pretend he is innocent.

Add. MSS. 47026, pp. 9-10

3 Disturbances on King William's Birthday, 1712

Dyer's Newsletter, 6 November 1712

Tuesday last being King William's birthday, the same by observation of it appeared as much forgotten as that of one of the Roman Caesars. However Jenny Man, the coffee woman at Charing Cross, had a bonfire at her door and there were some few others, but those who made the greatest noise were a knot of Whigs at the Three Tun Tavern in Grace Church Street, who brought a small mob with them [MS. torn] had a large bonfire made at the tavern door to whom they gave ale plentifully, and began disloyal healths and sung the song of Over Hanover, Over, etc. At which noise the Church Militant party came in, crying out 'the Whigs are for dethroning the Queen', routed their party that was about the bonfire and extinguished the same, broke the tavern windows, and had pulled down the house, but a party of the trained bands came in and prevented it. Since which my Lord Mayor has sent for the vintner and examined him who those persons were that made the riot and came down with their drawn swords into the street; but he would confess nothing, pretending that he did not know them though they had taken his balcony room for that purpose a fortnight ago. However they are known to be the same persons that lately made the like riot in Southampton Street. My Lord Mayor has bound over to the sessions Johnson the vintner and one Mr. Waterer, a Barbadoes merchant who bespoke the tavern room and the barrels of beer for the mob. This morning my Lord Mayor and the sheriffs were sent for by my Lord Bolingbroke [the Secretary of State] to give his Lordship an account of this matter.

Walton MSS. iv, 16

4 Street Warfare at the Bristol Election, 1713

Bristol, September 9th, 1713

On Monday the 7th instant our election came on and began about eight o'clock in the morning. The candidates were Sir William Daines, Joseph Earle, esquire, and Thomas Edwards, esquire. The people for Sir William Daines [the Whig candidate] desired St. George's Chapel and the entrance from thence into the Court, as usual; Mr. Edwards's friends having the Tailors' Hall (situate opposite to the Guild-Hall) to come from thence to give their votes. The passage abovementioned was refused to Sir William Daines's men, so that they must pass through the street into the Hall through a crowd and mob of the other side, placed on purpose to insult and knock them down, and thereby terrify them from coming to the poll. Before the poll begun, Lawford Cole, High Sheriff of the County of Gloucester, had got a considerable number of people in St. James's church yard, and there gave them a barrel of punch (a good preparative to keep the peace), and from thence marched them to the Tolzey and then to the Guild-Hall, with knots of ribbons in their hats for distinction.... Sir Will Daines's party adjourned to the Cooper's Hall, a place far distant, and thence brought their men to poll, but not without meeting with violent insults from the ribbon mob during the time of polling ... They were hurried out of the Hall without voting, abused by unbecoming words as villains, dogs, rogues, and such like opprobrious language too odious to be inserted; and when forced down, they fell to the mercy of the mob who were waiting for them. Whereupon, the day expiring, the court was adjourned to the next morning, seven o'clock, having polled in all but 334 men.

Against that time Sir William Daines's men ... did for their safety get about 500 men (all free voters) to defend their entrance into the Guild-

Hall, in order to poll; but before they got there the contrary party, seeing them so numerous and thereby able to defend themselves, capitulated, and promised solemnly to offer no disturbance for the future, desiring those men might be placed in convenient houses, to bring them gradually to poll ... But two hours after, Mr. Edwards's friends, having gathered all the people they could (among which were many colliers out of Kinswood and others that had no right to vote), thought fit to set them with flails in their hands before the places where Sir William Daines's men were lodged, and wholly prevented their coming out. ... The managers for Mr. Edwards took that opportunity to demand of the sheriffs to make proclamation for all persons that would vote for Sir William Daines to appear; but for the reasons above, none durst come in, although there were above 100 men in the above-said chapel adjoining the court, who locked themselves up for fear of being murdered. Upon which the sheriffs thought fit, at the demand of Mr. Edwards's friends, to proclaim the election, having polled in all but 660 men, whereas by a moderate computation there are 3600 free electors, all, or very nearly all, in the city, and ready to give their votes.

The Flying-Post, No. 3428, 15-17 Sept. 1713

L

WOMEN AND POLITICS

In the divided society of the years 1694-1716, and especially after 1701 when the issues between Whig and Tory became sharply delineated, many upper-class women took an eager interest in politics and were strongly partisan. Some were far more passionately involved than thousands of men who had the vote: it would have been hard, for instance, to find a more zealous Whig in London between 1709 and 1711 than that vehement anti-clerical, Lord Cowper's sister-in-law, Ann Clavering (4). A privileged few could even claim that they exercised some influence, however slight, on the fortunes of the parties.

L WOMEN AND POLITICS

This influence was not confined to the Court and the royal closet, though it is on this aspect of petticoat-politics that historians have traditionally dwelt. In fact it is an aspect whose importance has been much exaggerated. No woman influenced William III's judgement one iota after Mary's death in 1694. George I's German mistresses, though cultivated by aspiring Whig politicians in the years from 1714-16, were in no sense involved in *party* rivalry. By contrast, the three chief favourites at the court of Queen Anne, the Duchesses of Marlborough and Somerset and Abigail Masham, were all politically committed – the first two to the Whigs, the third to the Tories. Yet the reality of their influence over the Queen was often far removed from what party politicians imagined it to be. Sarah's championship of the Whigs in the early years of the reign, on her own admission, achieved little success until her pleas were reinforced by those of her husband and Lord Treasurer Godolphin. Yet many thought her the power behind the throne. A still greater myth grew up round the unprepossessing person of the woman who supplanted her in the royal favour (**S.6**). In January 1710, after Anne had promised the colonelship of the late Lord Essex's regiment of dragoons to Jack Hill, Mrs. Masham's Tory brother, Marlborough set the whole political world by the ears by offering the Queen a choice (which she calmly evaded) between his own services and those of the new favourite (**1, i**). The Whigs were equally dismayed, and some talked wildly of promoting an address from the Commons asking the Queen to remove from Court a woman whom they believed had the power to ruin them. Had they known how modestly Abigail herself rated her political influence (**1, ii**) they would never have contemplated so foolish a step.

If in the royal closet feminine influence was less than is often imagined, in parliamentary elections it was probably greater. Most of it was exercised backstage; but a few women controlled important electoral 'interests' in their own right, while the Duchess of Marlborough not merely canvassed voters openly at St. Albans in 1705 but engaged in political debate with some of them (**2**).

However, no event in this period aroused the interest and partisanship of women so thoroughly as the trial of Dr. Sacheverell, a public spectacle as well as a dramatic parade of party principles and loyalties. The special stands which Wren erected in Westminster Hall were half filled with ladies of fashion, eager and sometimes militant spectators of an event which, in its colour, its passion and its compensating humour, seemed to mirror the whole conflict of party in Augustan society (**3**).

1 Bedchamber Politics: The Influence of Abigail Masham

(i) The Duke of Marlborough to Queen Anne [20 January 1710]

By what I hear from London, I find your Majesty is pleased to think that, when I have reflected, I must be of opinion that you are in the right in giving Mr. Hill the Earl of Essex's regiment. I beg your Majesty will be so just to me as not to think I can be so unreasonable as to be mortified to the degree that I am, if it proceeded only from this one thing ... But this is only one of a great many mortifications that I have met with. And as I may not have many opportunities of writing to you, let me beg of your Majesty to reflect what your own people, and the rest of the world, must think, who have been witnesses of the love, zeal and duty with which I have served you, when they shall see that after all I have done it has not been able to protect me against the malice of a bedchamber woman. Your Majesty will allow me on this occasion to remind you of what I writ to you the last campaign, of the certain knowledge I had of Mrs. Masham's having assured Mr. Harley that I should receive such constant mortifications as should make it impossible for me to continue in your service.

God Almighty and the whole world are my witnesses, with what care and pains I have served you for more than twenty years, and I was resolved, if possible, to have struggled with the difficulties to the end of this war. But the many instances I have had of your Majesty's great change to me has so broke my spirits that I must beg, as the greatest and last favour, that you will approve of my retiring, so that I may employ the little time I have to live in making my just acknowledgements to God for the protection he has been pleased to give me ...

An Account of the Conduct of the Dowager Duchess of Marlborough (1742), pp. 232-4

(ii) Abigail Masham to Robert Harley, 10 March 1710

Last night I had a great deal of discourse with my aunt [the Queen] and much of it about the two men that are named for bishops. I told her what a wild character Barton had, and that her father never made a worse man one than he is. She said very little to me, but by what she did say I suspect from it she has promised he shall be one as well as Bradford ... Now nobody can serve her if she goes on privately doing these things every day, when she has had so much said to her as I know she has, both from myself and other people; and because am I still with her people think I am able to persuade her to anything I have a mind to have her do, but they will be convinced to the contrary one time or other. I desired her to let me see you. She would not consent to that, and charged me not to say anything to you of what passed between us. She is angry with me and said I was in a passion. Perhaps I might speak a little too warm, but who can help that when one sees plainly she is giving her best friends up to the rage of their enemies. I have had no rest this night, my concern is so great; and for my part I should be glad to leave my aunt before I am forced from her ...

Hist. MSS. Comm. *Portland MSS.* iv, 536

2 The Duchess of Marlborough's Electioneering at St. Albans, 1705

Upon the petition of Henry Killigrew, esquire, complaining of an undue election and return of John Gape, esquire, to serve for the borough of St. Albans ...

The sitting member's counsel ... insisted on several irregular practices on behalf of the petitioner; and as to that they called several witnesses.

Charles Turner said he was sent for by the Duchess of Marlborough; and he went to her, and she desired his vote for both admirals [Killigrew and Churchill]: that he answered, he was engaged for Mr. Gape; to which the Duchess replied, she had no prejudice to Mr. Gape, but it was the Queen's desire that no such men should be chose, for such men would unhinge the government, and the Papists' horses stood saddled day and night, whipping and spurring.

John Miller said that he was asked by one to go to my Lady Marlborough's; and when he came the Duchess asked him who he was for, and he answered, for Colonel (*sic*) Churchill and Mr. Gape. Thereupon the duchess asked him if he would be for such men as were against the Queen's interest and the good of the nation?; that she asked him to oblige her with one vote; and he said, he thought he did by giving her brother one.

Jeremy Hopkins said the Duchess of Marlborough sent for him; and when he came she desired to know who he was for: that he told her he had promised to be for Mr. Gape and her brother; to which she replied that she had nothing to say against Mr. Gape, but Tackers (**M(d).2, iv**) would be injurious to the government and were for the French interest; and upon that occasion she read over to him King Charles the 2nd's speech against tacking...

John Wilkinson, William Gibson, John Cole, clerk, and Dr. John Cootsworth gave also an account that the Duchess had sent for them and desired their votes for Mr. Killigrew; and when they told her they were engaged for Mr. Gape she said she was sorry for it. Only Dr. Cootsworth gave some account of a discourse that the Duchess and he had together, *pro* and *con*, as to several points of state.

Commons' Journals, xv, 38

3 Women and the Sacheverell Trial, 1710

(i) Sir John Perceval to Philip Perceval, 2 March 1710

Tuesday night we sat by two ladies at the trial who fell out, being of different sides, and had certainly fought, but the mother of one of them pulled her daughter away and carried her home. She wondered how the other could justify so wicked a man; besides madam (said she), he is not a bit handsome... My Lady Rooke is a heroine in his behalf. She was t'other day eating some cold chicken in the Hall[1] and gave a wing to a gentleman who sat by her. But it coming into her head to ask him if he was for Sacheverell, and he answering, no by G-d madam, then by G-d sir, said she, I will have my wing again, and snatch it out of his hands.

Add. MSS. 47026, pp. 10-12

(ii) Ann Clavering to James Clavering, 23 March 1710

To cheer your drooping spirits I must conclude with a story of the Duke of Richmond... The Duchess of Cleveland told her Duke he was to vote for the Doctor, and speak as his brother Northumberland did; to which end of Monday she lock him up, and bid the servants tell the Duke of Richmond he was gone out (fearing him). The Duke comes; the servants obey the Duchess's commands; his Grace, not satisfied, lights out of his coach, run[s] over the house, meets with one room locked, calls, and was answered, I'm here, but can't get out, my wife's

---

[1] Westminster Hall, the scene of the trial.

locked me up; to which the Duke [of] Richmond says, I'll release you. Away he runs; fetches a ladder, set[s] it to the window, take[s] the Duke out and put[s] him in his coach; and bids him say in the House as he did, for he'd speak loud, which I can witness was observed. The former part I don't aver. However, 'tis a good story.

Durham University Library, Clavering Letters

4 A Whig Cameo: Ann Clavering

Ann to James Clavering, 1 April 1710

... The parsons are not [weary] of thundering out their ecclesiastical anathemas, for a young Oxo. last Sunday at the Temple said, no prince on earth had power to call God['s] Vicegerents (for so he styled the parsons) to account on any score; their power was from a more supreme being, etc; [and] so went on. At last, says this Moses for meekness, the primitive moderation was allowable, but for this modern moderation, if I understand my business, 'tis a damnable sin. I've the consolation yet from this doctrine that now they've rope enough they'll hang themselves ...

Now I must tell you I was lately myself insulted on this occasion. I went to make a visit where the picture of the Perjured Priest [Sacheverell] was, which put Lady Ann into a raving fit. I left nothing unsaid that could, I thought, provoke. At last I was told in derision, if you are so warm and fiery you'll never get a husband. O madam, says I, you mistake that matter. I despise all Tories, and were their estates never so large; and yet don't despair, for I am sure the Whigs like me better for being true to my party; and so we parted.

The Perjured Priest read prayers at his own church of Sunday morning, where there were such numbers of the mob that those near him kissed his hand. Others touched his garments and were blessed ... But here I must quit the parsons; I am weary of them.

Durham University Library, Clavering Letters

PART III *The Substance of Conflict*

M

ISSUES

Post-Revolution society was divided first and foremost over issues. Some of these were traditional areas of dispute between Whigs and Tories dating back to the reign of Charles II, though the configuration of the contested ground had naturally changed in certain respects between 1679 and 1694, and it changed further between 1694 and 1716. The coming of 'Dutch William' to the throne, however, confronted English politicians with many new problems. Overshadowing all the rest was the fact that revolution at home led to a revolution – no less far-reaching in its consequences – in England's relations with Europe. The issues raised by this new relationship extended the field of domestic conflict well beyond its original limits.

(a) *War and Foreign Policy*

William III's foreign policy, which was also the policy of Queen Anne's principal advisers between 1702 and 1710, involved England's commitment to a Continental alliance-system designed to achieve two great ends: to prevent the hegemony of Louis XIV of France, and to restore a balance of power in Europe beween the dynastic houses of Bourbon and Habsburg. Among its more specific objectives were to secure the Protestant line and the Protestant religion in England (for Louis was the chief support of the exiled Catholic Stuarts); to protect the vulnerable frontier of the United Provinces by means of a 'Barrier'

M (a) WAR AND FOREIGN POLICY 89

– a line of fortresses in the Spanish Netherlands which the Dutch would have the right to garrison; and after 1700, when Louis' grandson succeeded to the throne of Spain, to recover for the maritime powers their former trade with Spanish territories in the Old and New Worlds. Defensive though it was in conception, the new foreign policy seemed startlingly ambitious to seventeenth century eyes. Some of its implications – notably the undertaking in 1703 to depose the Bourbon King of Spain and impose a German Habsburg[1] on a largely unwilling nation in his stead – were ambitious by any standards. Above all it was an exhausting and expensive policy; for as William III found to his cost after 1697 France could not be contained by mere diplomacy, only by a prolonged effort of arms.

Since only Parliament could underwrite a policy so costly and far-reaching, the issues to which it gave rise naturally became matters for debate and controversy between the parliamentary parties. By the years 1694–7 two opposing positions were already discernible, the one generally critical of the new trends and taken up by the great majority of Tories, the other more favourably disposed and held by the ministerial Whigs, especially by those associated with the Junto. Down to 1701, however, a good deal of common ground remained between the parties. Country Whigs as well as Tories clamoured for the reduction of the standing army in 1698–9 (**M(b).3, P.2**) and it required the fresh shock of the Spanish Succession crisis in 1701–2 to dispel the euphoria induced by the compromise Peace of Ryswick (1697) and to reconcile the Whig party as a whole to the full implications of a Williamist foreign policy and war strategy (**C**).

From then on attitudes became strongly defined. The Whigs accepted the necessity for a renewal of the war enthusiastically and confidently, and supported first William and later Marlborough and Godolphin in committing England to the role of a 'principal' in the Grand Alliance (**1**). The Tories lent their backing to the war belatedly, grudgingly and apprehensively. Even the powerful new commercial arguments in favour of renewing hostilities, let alone the religious and dynastic *causes de guerre*, left some of them unimpressed, and early setbacks suffered by the Alliance from 1702–4 gave Tory jeremiahs perverse satisfaction (**1, 2**).

Behind these attitudes lay a basic difference in outlook. The Whigs were conscious of the interdependence of England and the Continent, and were ready to shoulder the responsibilities which a close involve-

[1] Archduke Charles, second son of Emperor Leopold I, crowned Charles III of Spain in 1706.

ment in European affairs entailed (**6, ii**). The old guard of the Tory party, represented by Lord Rochester and Sir Edward Seymour, and most of its independent country gentlemen, were frankly isolationist. Even the party's new recruits, led by Harley and St. John, came to favour a policy of partial disengagement, with the Balance of Power maintained by diplomacy or, as a last resort, by a limited, naval war (**5**). To the average Tory, alliances were disagreeable necessities and allies automatic objects of suspicion. Not surprisingly, in view of the experience of William III's reign, this antipathy became especially fierce in the case of the Dutch.

The Barrier Treaty of 1709, in which the Whigs held out to the United Provinces, as bait to keep them in the war, far greater rewards in the final settlement than even William III had ever envisaged, was denounced by Tory propagandists (**4**) and revoked (1712) by a Tory ministry. It was regarded by half the political nation as the most shameful symbol of a foreign policy which (as they saw it) allowed the wealth and manpower of England to be drained year after year to aggrandise her Continental neighbours and to maintain their Whig friends in power at home.

From these preconceptions and prejudices two further consequences naturally flowed.

1. Tory notions of war strategy clashed with those of the Whigs. The vast majority of Tories opposed the maintenance of a large army in Flanders, to which first William and then Marlborough gave priority. Instead they either favoured an 'auxiliary' role for England, with the emphasis on maritime and colonial operations (**S.3**) or preferred, after the treaty with Portugal in 1703, to regard the Peninsula as the most important sphere of land warfare. After the Almanza disaster in 1707 a favourite Tory proposal was that a third or so of Marlborough's troops in Flanders should be transferred to Spain; even the final humiliation of the battle of Brihuega (1710) did not entirely kill this idea, one that never failed to horrify the Whigs (**3**).

2. It was the Tories who both led and profited from the agitation for peace in England in the years 1709-13. Not that their leaders were for peace at any price. But they had far fewer scruples than the Whigs about neglecting the interests of the allies, and after the summer of 1710 they were swept along by powerful currents of feeling in the country into the policies of abandoning Spain to the Bourbons and privately negotiating with France, which led to the Utrecht treaties of 1713-14. Even then, Lord Oxford's claim in 1714 that the settlement was 'an honourable and advantageous peace' for Britain (**5**) was at least half

true, and the Whigs later tacitly conceded this by treating the settlement as one of the cornerstones of their own foreign policy after 1714.

The Whig ministry of 1714-16 also set itself to repair the alliance-system which the Tories had so rudely unhinged, and even to associate their old enemy with it after Louis XIV's death in 1715. When, however, George I's German interests threatened to involve Britain in a Balance of Power policy in the north as well as in the west and south of Europe, even such good Europeans as Lord Townshend demurred; and by a curious irony disagreement on this issue proved a major cause of the Whig schism of 1717 (**6**).

1 A Tory Merchant's Opinion of William III's Foreign Policy, 1701

Henry Whistler to Governor Thomas Pitt, 20 December 1701

Under pretence to carry on their party they [the Whigs] cry up a war with Spain and France, and to join with the Dutch and Emperor to take Spain from the present new King for the Emperor, pretending that France and Spain being joined in one family we shall lose all our trade with Spain and in the Straits. Upon this fear we are mad[e] to make a war with both, and to beat them into better manners, and to force them to the continuance of wearing baize cloaks and other commodities of ours. All this is the present cry, not considering that the same day we make war we lose all for the time of war in hopes of the future, which to me is madness; for by war the French will gain the trade and bring them to wear their commodities, and they by a present aversion to us will get into a habit of wearing the French goods, and we shall never get them out of it, I fear. Our King and the States of Holland have both owned the King of Spain, but after doing it have thought good to repent it, and to put fears and jealousies into our heads that the French King, having the sole governing of the new King of Spain, will invade Holland. Upon this a confederacy is made betwixt the Emperor and the States to conquer Spain and set up the Emperor's title. To this end an army was sent into Italy under Prince Eugene to take Milan . . .

At the sitting of the last Parliament the Dutch sent a memorial to the King which he communicated to the House, showing their danger of being invaded by the French, they having men in all the garrisons of

Flanders and by it being masters of all the Barriers, and prayed the King's assistance. Upon this the House had a very long debate. The Court party were for us to come in as principals in the war, but the House would go no further than to assist the States General in keeping of Holland and the peace of Europe, and to that end to send them 10,000 men and to pay them, which is done. The States have had at least 100,000 men this summer in the field but as yet have done no act of hostility, nor the French nor Spaniard, for at present you must observe we call all things done in Spain as if done by the French. The temper of the last Parliament saved us last year from a war, and we have got home great riches by it that we must have lost in a war, but for this they are arraigned by many that hoped to have gained by a war and that it might divert the storm from the late [Whig] ministry.

Add. MSS. 22851, fos. 131-2

2 The Spanish Succession War through Tory Eyes, 1703

Sir Miles Warton to Thomas Pitt, 14 April 1703

To give you a little of our news: we are prosecuting a war against France and Spain, a legacy the late King left us; but we are at the old play we were in his time of pulling down France, and are ourselves in more danger of being pulled down. The Elector of Bavaria is of the French side, at the head of his army in the Empire, and carries all before him. The war of Italy the French have got the superiority. Our army in Flanders under the duke of Marlborough is now going to besiege Bonn. The Dutch have scrambled up a pretty good frontier; when they have had enough I hope we shall have peace . . .

Add. MSS. 22852, fo. 63

3 Flanders versus Spain: The Commons' Debate on the Queen's Message concerning the Defeat at Brihuega, 1711

Mungo Graham to the Duke of Montrose, 2 January 1711

[Mr. St. John, after delivering the message, said] her Majesty would take all proper measures for supporting that [Spanish] war, for the

3 FLANDERS VERSUS SPAIN: THE COMMONS' DEBATE, 1711

maintaining of which this Parliament had shown their inclinations so early. Mr. Freeman [Tory M.P. for Hertfordshire] spoke next, and concluded with a motion that an humble address should be presented to her Majesty returning the thanks of the House for her most gracious message, and for her great care and conduct in making such effectual provisions for that war, and that they will enable her Majesty to make effectual such measures as she, in her great wisdom, shall think necessary for retrieving the late losses in Spain and for carrying on the war in all its parts with vigour. This was seconded by two or three more.

Then Wortley Montagu [Whig M.P. for Huntingdon] spoke, and, as I thought, very unseasonably insinuated a distrust he had from that motion that the intention was to strengthen the war in Spain by weakening the army in Flanders. However Mr. Walpole, some time after, said that he was glad to hear that the measures which had been concerted for carrying on the war in Spain were put in a right way, as he thought, viz. by hiring foreign troops and sending them from Italy, which in many respects he thought was the most effectual way of doing it. But that there having been so much talking without doors as if that was to be carried on by sending troops from Flanders (which, by the by, he said could not be done without breaking the treaties of the alliance), and that the words of this address being general (as indeed the message was), he was afraid it might be interpreted afterwards as if the House had given their opinion in a matter which was not then in their view; and therefore proposed an amendment to the motion, viz. these words (in concert with the allies), that's to say, such measures as her Majesty in concert with the allies, etc.

Then Mr. Harley said that the message was general, and could not otherways be, because no particular information was yet come; and if the message was general, the address fell very naturally to be such. That he was sorry that anything should have been so much as hinted at in that House, as if there was any design not to keep up the terms of the treaties of alliance, or that the war in Flanders was to be neglected ... Then Lieutenant General Webb [Tory M.P. for Ludgershall] made a speech which disconcerted all that had been said before and gave Mr. Walpole's friends a very good handle to justify his proposal. He said that everybody was sensible that in all this war the war in Spain had been starved, and that in Flanders very sufficiently provided for; and that in his opinion the war in Spain could not be well maintained by sending such troops as were usually sent there, but that it would be necessary to send the very best of the troops they had for that service;

and that if 20 battalions of the best troops in Flanders were sent it would soon be seen what a change of affairs they would make; and [he] said that he wished that those who have been knocked in the head there this last year unnecessarily had been sent to Spain. This gave an opportunity for Sir Joseph Jekyll [Whig M.P. for Eye] to say that what Mr. Walpole had said was not so far out of the road as was pretended ...

Scottish Record Office, Montrose MSS.

4 The Attack on the Barrier Treaty, 1712

Imagine a reasonable person in China reading the [Barrier] treaty, and one who was ignorant of our affairs or our geography. He would conceive their High Mightinesses the States-General to be some vast powerful commonwealth, like that of Rome, and her Majesty to be a petty prince, like one of those to whom that republic would sometimes send a diadem for a present, when they behaved themselves well, otherwise could depose at pleasure and place whom they thought fit in their stead. Such a man would think that the States had taken our prince and us into their protection, and in return honoured us so far as to make use of our troops as some small assistance in their conquests and the enlargement of their empire, or to prevent the incursions of barbarians upon some of their outlying provinces.

But how must it sound in a European ear that Great Britain, after maintaining a war for so many years with so much glory and success and such prodigious expense, after saving the Empire, Holland and Portugal, and almost recovering Spain, should toward the close of a war enter into a treaty with seven Dutch provinces to secure to them a dominion larger than their own, which she had conquered for them; ... and accept as an equivalent the mean condition of those States assisting to preserve her Queen on the throne, whom, by God's assistance, she is able to defend against all her Majesty's enemies and allies put together?

Such a wild bargain could never have been made for us if the States had not found it their interest to use very powerful motives with the chief advisers (I say nothing of the person immediately employed [Lord Townshend]), and if a party here at home had not been resolved, for ends and purposes very well known, to continue the war as long as they had any occasion for it ...

4 THE ATTACK ON THE BARRIER TREATY, 1712

It is no doubt for the interest of Britain that the States should have a sufficient barrier against France; but their High Mightinesses, for some few years past, have put a different meaning upon the word barrier from what it formerly used to bear when applied to them... In the Grand Alliance of 1701 the several powers promising to endeavour to recover Flanders for a barrier was understood to be the recovering of those provinces to the King of Spain. But in this treaty the style is wholly changed. Here are about twenty towns and forts of great importance, with their chattellanies and dependencies... and the whole revenues of them to be under the perpetual military government of the Dutch, by which that republic will be entirely masters of the richest part of all Flanders, and upon any appearance of war they may put their garrisons into any other place of the Low Countries...

Let us consider the consequences of our triumphs, upon which some set so great a value as to think that nothing less than the crown can be a sufficient reward for the merit of the general. We have not enlarged our dominions by one foot of land; our trade, which made us considerable in the world, is either given up by treaties or clogged with duties, which interrupt and daily lessen it. We see the whole nation groaning under excessive taxes of all sorts to raise three millions of money for payment of the interest of those debts we have contracted. Let us look upon the reverse of the medal. We shall see our neighbours, who in their utmost distress called for our assistance, become by this treaty, even in time of peace, masters of a more considerable country than their own; in a condition to strike terror into us, with fifty thousand veterans ready to invade us from that country which we have conquered for them.[1]

Jonathan Swift, Some Remarks on the Barrier Treaty (1712)

5 Principles of Tory Foreign Policy after the Spanish Succession War

Lord Oxford's Draft for the Queen's Speech at the Opening of the 1714 Session

---

[1] A reference to Article 2 of the Barrier Treaty, by which the States-General undertook to guarantee the Hanoverian Succession in Britain, by armed assistance if necessary – a provision particularly obnoxious to the Tories.

19 February 1714

My Lords and Gentlemen,

I have great satisfaction in being able at the opening of this Parliament to tell you that the ratifications of the Treaties of Peace and Commerce with Spain are exchanged, by which my subjects will have greater opportunites than ever to extend and improve their trade. Many of the advantages enjoyed by connivance only, contrary to the laws of that country, and by such methods as made a distinction between one British merchant and another, are now settled by treaty and made an equal rule to all my subjects.

God has thus blessed my endeavours to procure an honourable and advantageous peace to my own subjects and the greatest part of our allies. My best endeavours shall not be wanting to rescue others from the calamity of war, and I have reason to promise myself success therein.

In the meantime it is with great pleasure I see my subjects delivered from a consuming war, and entering upon such a peace as nothing but their own *intestine broils* can hinder the effects of it in an universal increase of trade.

And in this [I have set before me for my rule][1] the example of those of my predecessors who have been most renowned for their wisdom and for their love and care of their subjects. They made it their practice and their maxim to hold the balance between the contending powers of Europe, to be the peace-makers, and by managing of it so that where Britain cast in the weight, that gave the preference.

This made us really formidable abroad, and brought riches home, and is what God and nature by our situation has pointed out to be our true interest; and it is that rule which never has been departed from but when faction had turned men's heads from the love of their country to pursue imaginary schemes of government or their private lucre. And as I have [made] this maxim the aim of my government, so I doubt not but my Protestant successors will think it their glory to pursue the same, for it [is] this nation's interest to aggrandise itself by trade, and when a war is necessary it is their interest as well as safety to carry it on by sea.

Brit. Mus. Loan 29/7, folder 6

---

[1] Alternative version suggested by Oxford.

6 The Whigs and 'The Balance of the North', 1716

(i) Lord Townshend to James Stanhope, 16 October 1716

The miserable and distracted condition into which the northern affair are plunged gives the discontented and enemies of the King's government hopes that they may be able to raise some disturbances in Parliament on that head, which they flatter themselves may be managed so as to affect the King's affairs in general; and indeed I cannot but own their expectations in this particular to be better founded, and their schemes more wisely laid, than they use to be ... Mr. Lechmere and some other Whigs, as I am credibly informed, are to take their share; and your humble servant and yourself are personally to suffer in this attack, *tho' God knows we have had no direction in all this northern quarrel* ...

I perfectly agree with you that England, as well as the rest of Europe veer had and always must have a great interest in the preservation of the balance of the north; and yet I cannot help being of opinion that if the northern affairs were brought into Parliament by his Majesty's order upon the foot they now stand his Majesty would be so far from obtaining any assistance on that head that there would be great danger from such a step of ruining his credit and influence in both Houses ... I suppose by supporting the balance of the north it is now meant both against the Czar and Sweden; and I doubt very much whether any scheme of that kind can be displayed in such colours as to invite the Parliament to engage in it. For besides the difficulties our trade must lie under, should we actually break with the Czar, the expense necessary to support such a scheme will be an insuperable reason with the Parliament never to come into it.

(ii) The Earl of Sunderland to Lord Townshend, Gohre, [31 October] 1716

... I must not omit ... acquainting your Lordship that the King is very much surprised at the strange notion that seems at present to prevail, as if the Parliament was not to concern themselves in anything that happens in these parts of the world, which he looks upon not only as exposing him to all kinds of affronts, but even to ruin: and indeed this notion is nothing but the old Tory one, that England can subsist by itself, whatever becomes of the rest of Europe, which has been so justly exploded ever since the Revolution.

Coxe, *Walpole*, ii, 118-19, 128

(b) Government and Monarchy

In the great seventeenth-century debate about the basis of kingship and the nature of government the pre-Revolution Whigs and Tories had taken opposite sides at every crucial point: over hereditary right, over the questions of obedience and resistance to the king, over the so-called 'contract', over the prerogative. Then came the events of 1688-9, when most Tories disavowed the High Anglican political creed, either by active rebellion or passive acquiescence in the consequences of rebellion. Logically these events should have put an end to the debate about government and monarchy. Yet up to a point the debate continued in spite of them.

Criticism or defence of the royal prerogative, it is true, were no longer valid marks of distinction between Whigs and Tories in the years 1694-1716. In William's reign, when the powers of the Crown were still considerable, many of their most vociferous critics were Tories, the very men who had upheld the prerogative in the 70's and 80's. In the standing army controversy of 1697-9 Whig leaders were forced by a sense of ministerial responsibility into defending a traditional object of Whig suspicion (3). Nevertheless the reputation of the Whigs for hostility to the prerogative, not least in the field of ministerial appointments, lingered on into the early eighteenth century. It prejudiced Queen Anne against them (4), and it made even George I wary at first of their professions.

By contrast, the argument over hereditary right retained its relevance, even after William of Orange had succeeded to the throne in stark defiance of the hereditary principle. Save for the scruples of a small minority, the Tory conscience was reconciled to the 1689 settlement by four circumstances. It was soothed because Princess Mary, James II's eldest daughter, was crowned along with her husband; because William's subjects were neither expected to recognise him as King *de jure* nor take an oath abjuring all allegiance to James; and because of the provision that, failing the birth of an heir to Mary, the succession would still devolve through the female Stuart line through Princess Anne to her one surviving son, the Duke of Gloucester. The removal of three of these four anodynes one by one between Mary's death in 1694 and William's in 1702 was a painful process (**M (c).2**). However, the bulk of the Tories possessed both a healthy instinct of self-preservation and a saving capacity for self-deception, and together these qualities saw them through each crisis. They were especially exemplified in the party's reaction to the discovery of a plot to assassinate the

King in 1696 and to the Whig demand that all members of Parliament should subscribe to an Association to defend their 'rightful and lawful' monarch (**1**). But they were again in evidence during the progress of the Bill of Settlement through Parliament, following the death of the Duke of Gloucester (**C.3**), and after Louis XIV's recognition of the Pretender as James III of England (1701), which enabled William and the Whigs to insist at last on the imposition of an Abjuration oath on members and officials. It was not surprising that the Tories took fresh heart at Anne's accession, since this enabled them to postpone their final crisis of conscience still longer (**2, i**). Jacobites and crypto-Jacobites soon grew accustomed to taking the new oaths tongue in cheek (**2, ii**); but the arguments voiced during the trial of Sacheverell in 1710 proved that the notion of hereditary right was far from being dead and buried, and they foreshadowed the remarkable revival of Jacobitism in Anne's closing years.

The Sacheverell trial also offered the Whigs an opportunity to hold a full-dress parade of 'revolution principles'. They were able to reaffirm not merely their acceptance of parliamentary right and 'contract' monarchy but their rejection of non-resistance and passive obedience. Their views on the right of resistance were not popular in 1710; and as many Whigs foresaw, they recoiled on them at the next Election, when charges of holding anti-monarchical and even republican opinions were hurled at their heads (**6**). But as a fundamental article of party faith such views still had an obvious practical relevance. No one could doubt after 1710 that if the Pretender usurped the crown after Anne's death, in subversion of the law, the Whigs at least would resist him with complete conviction (**5**).

1 The Reception of the Association, 1696

(i) When by these examinations the matter [of the assassination plot] was clear and undeniable, the King communicated it in a speech to both Houses of Parliament... Motions were made in both Houses for an Association, wherein they should own him as their rightful and lawful king, and promise faithfully to adhere to him against King James and the pretended Prince of Wales; engaging at the same time to maintain the act of succession, and to revenge his death on all who should be concerned in it.

This was much opposed in both Houses, chiefly by Seymour and Finch in the House of Commons and the Earl of Nottingham in the House of

Lords. They went chiefly upon this: that *rightful* and *lawful* were word that had been laid aside in the beginning of this reign; that they imported one that was king by descent, and so could not belong to the present king. They said, the crown and the prerogatives of it were vested in him, and therefore they would obey him and be faithful to him, though they could not acknowledge him their rightful and lawful king ...

After a warm debate it was carried in both Houses that an Association should be laid on the table, and that it might be signed by all such as were willing of their own accord to sign it; only with this difference, that instead of the words '*rightful* and *lawful* king' the Lords put these words: 'that King William hath the right by law to the crown of these realms, and that neither King James, nor the pretended Prince of Wales, nor any other person has any right whatsoever to the same'. This was done to satisfy those who said they could not come up to the words *rightful* and *lawful*; and the Earl of Rochester offering these words,[1] they were thought to answer the ends of the Association, and so were agreed to. This was signed by both Houses, excepting olny four score in the House of Commons and fifteen in the House of Lords.[2] The Association was carried from the Houses of Parliament over all England, and was signed by all sorts of people, a very few only excepted.

Own Time, iv, 305-7

(ii) [Robert Harley] to William Bromley, 28 April 1696 (copy)

Our friend Sir Ch[ristopher] M[usgrave][3] began his journey yesterday morning to the north. He made it his business by all arguments to persuade his friends to sign ... [The] continuance of this Parliament seems (at present) resolved. The aim for that and other advices will be taken from the proceedings of the non-subscribers, the expectation being whether they will give encouragement to their friends by subscribing at midsummer sessions in their several counties, or gratify their enemies (with the public damage) by refusing on Friday. I hear there will be a general meeting of the non-subscribers to consider of this matter, and the inclination of those I converse with seems to be for compliance with the law, having distinguished their principles enough by not doing that voluntarily, which receives a different character when it is required by law ...

---

[1] The proposal actually came from the Duke of Leeds (the former Earl of Danby).
[2] Burnet understated the size of the Tory protest. There were about 100 refusals in the Commons and about 20 in the Lords.
[3] Tory M.P. for Appleby.

I have met with some who have taken pains with great niceness and scrupulosity to examine this for their own satisfaction, and they tell me that by all they can find in Bishop Sanderson, Grotius and others ... there is no ground of doubt from the words themselves to any person who hath taken the Oath of Allegiance. Since the Act of Recognition in the first session of last Parliament, custom hath made other parts of the title, vizt., King of France and Defender of the Faith, familiar, and therefore nobody studies objections or scruples; and should the law make additions of Caesar Augustus, vestra aeternitas, as well as Majestas, which have been given to Emperors, the scrupling such a compliance would only call in question the person's judgement, unless he had a good force to support his denial.

But I beg pardon for all this stuff to a person of so great reading, good sense and well poised judgement as Mr. Bromley, ... whose love to his country and the public good (so nearly concerned at this question) supersedes all the arguments of (otherwise) just resentments ...; but I am sure you will sacrifice more than that to the preserving the whole and keeping the nation from the power of a party who can have no strength but what is given them by such a refusal. Therefore I hope we shall be preserved by you from having stripes by scourges cut out of our own skins.

Brit. Mus. Loan 29/188

2 The Tories and the Abjuration Oath, 1702

(i) Viscount Weymouth to Hon. James Thynne, Chilton, 27 March 1702

Though I wrote so lately to my dear brother, I am willing to trouble you again with the account of my design for home tomorrow, and that neither you nor brother H. may forbear taking measures till you know mine. I hasten to tell you both, that though I have not absolutely resolved to take this new Oath, yet I have read and discoursed so much with the most knowing and honest men about it, that I am much nearer doing it than I ever thought I should be, and may possibly submit to do it, the case being so much altered by the death of King William, and the old as well as new laws being on the Queen's side. And if conscience will allow it, I am sure prudence will prompt to strengthen her government, and restore the Church to the ground it has lost.

Longleat MSS. Thynne Papers, xiii, fo. 287

(ii) Charles Cox to John Gellibrand, Southwark, 24 February 1705

I must confess what is reported of a discourse between Mr. Lade and myself is true, which is, that about four years since, he and I talking something warmly about the pretended P[rince] of W[ales], his legitimacy, and possibility of his accession to the throne, after long disputes he affirmed that when we had done all we must have the young gentleman again; to which I replied, then we are all ruined, or to that purpose. Further, councillor Martin our Bailiff told me that, since this, Mr. Lade told him near the Temple that his friends, meaning the Jacks, were milksops for kicking at oaths, asserting they should never be able to do anything if they, his friends, did not take all oaths that could be imposed; but I hope the nation is out of danger from any ill practices from the prostitution of oaths.

Blenheim MSS. D.1-32

3 The Whigs and the Prerogative: The Standing Army Controversy of 1697-9

[Simon Clement], *Faults on Both Sides* (1710)

... What will fix a perpetual mark of infamy on the heads of that Whig ministry is, that (being under apprehensions that they should be laid by after the peace) they were the men who entered into a compact with King William, that if he would keep them and their friends in his ministry, they would use their interest in the House of Commons to procure him a standing army of twenty thousand men. And though in this worse than Tory attempt, the wise and honest men of their party deserted them, and they could not carry their point, yet they struggled hard to keep up as many of the Army as possible, and dispersed pamphlets to persuade the silly people among their own party that forces kept up from year to year by consent of Parliament were not to be accounted a standing army, and that the great number of forces continued by the French king, and I know not what other circumstances, made it absolutely necessary for a time; nay they have insulted (*sic*) since the short duration of the peace, and would have it thought they were in the right, and that none but King William's enemies were for disbanding the army. But all this is odious language from the mouth of a Whig, with whom it should be a maxim never to be departed from, not to trust the Crown with any such overbalance of power as can enable it to endanger the liberties of the nation.

2nd edn., pp. 20-21

4 The Whigs and the Prerogative: The Fears of Queen Anne, 1708

The Queen to the Duke of Marlborough [endorsed 27 August 1708]

Lord Treasurer has gone to make a visit to the Bishop of Ely, where the Town says he will meet with four or five gentlemen [of the Whig Junto], who I can never be satisfied mean well to my service till they behave themselves better than they did in the last Parliament, and have done ever since the rising of it. For from that minute they have been disputing my authority, and certainly designing, when the new one meets, to tear that little prerogative the Crown has to pieces. And now, because my servants and I set up one they formerly liked [Sir Richard Onslow] to be Speaker, they are against him; for no other reason, I suppose, but because they will have none in any employment that does not entirely depend upon them. Now how is it possible, when one knows and sees all these things as plainly as the sun at noon-day, ever to take these people into my bosom? For God's sake, do but make it your own case, and consider then what you would do, and why a handful of men must awe their fellow-subjects. There is nobody more desirous than I to encourage those Whig friends that behave themselves well; but ... to be short, I think things are come to [this], whether I shall submit to the five tyrannising lords, or they to me.

W. Coxe, *Memoirs of the Duke of Marlborough* (Bohn, 1848), ii, 292

5 A Whig Definition of the Right of Resistance, 1710

Robert Molesworth to Lord Godolphin, 8 March 1710

A king of England differs from a tyrant in this, that he has the executive power of the laws lodged in him by the constitution, and therefore when he puts to death, imprisons, fines or banishes any man he can do no wrong, because he does it in execution of those laws; and is not so much as supposed to act as a king upon any other foot. For the laws are such as are made by mutual consent, and if my representatives have agreed to such a law which 'tis my fault or unhappiness to have transgressed, I have no right to complain, much less to resist the executive power of the prince who punishes me for the breach of that law: and therefore the king does me no wrong; nor can do it, for 'tis not in his power to do wrong as a king. As a tyrant he may indeed do it ... as when he lies with my wife or daughter, or maims or imprisons me, not for breach of any law; but even in this case of private injuries ... I am not to endeavour to repel force with force so as to hurt his person, because the good of the Public is always to be my primary consideration. But if the constitution be invaded, if the laws be rendered only dead letters, if the interest of the nation be so visibly interested that a dissolution of the government is likely to ensue, then this king loses that name and becomes to all intents and purposes a general tyrant and has no right to anyone's either active or passive obedience. And after all that can be said of it, to speak the truth plainly and openly, the people who feel the grievances are the only and proper judges in this case: all other distinctions and subterfuges are notional, not to say nonsensical.

Blenheim MSS. B.2-33

6 A Warning to the Voters of Cockermouth not to choose Whigs, 1710

'Phill Ecclesiasto' to 'the person it may concern', 25 September 1710

We can't but be very surprised and concerned to hear [that] a man of your temper, sense and (as we hoped) well affected to the Established Church should at this time so far start aside as to associate with separatists and schismatics and assisting of them in the choice of members for the next British Parliament, as if that party were not strong enough already with the help of their Scotch friends, peers, commissioners and representatives ... Though his Grace my Lord Duke [of Somerset] himself (who has been a very bountiful benefactor to your borough) should now knowingly recommend to you a person of republican principles [James Stanhope], one that would not allow her present Majesty any hereditary title, that would be for clipping and paring the prerogative of the Crown, and for the erecting new schemes of government in order to ruin and undermine our present happy constitution

6 A WARNING TO THE VOTERS OF COCKERMOUTH, 1710

and establishment in Church and State, ... can you think yourself under any obligation to make choice of men for your representatives whom you have any reason to fear are of such dangerous principles? As for my Lord Wharton ... they always have him sure both upon principles and interest, and they need not fear his deceiving of them by his recommending any of contrary sentiments. It's true that both these great lords have been wonderfully kind to your town. What, then? Are you for that obliged to sacrifice your conscience? ...

The Queen, God bless her, no doubt has very good reasons for the changes she made in her ministers of state and for the dissolution of the Parliament. Many think she has been long under a kind of restraint and no free agent (not to say insulted) in the throne, and that she found her sacred person, crown and dignity in danger from men of base disloyal and republican principles. If so, where is the prudence, policy or good manners to her Majesty or our nation to promote to the interest and design of such who may again distress her and all her good subjects?

Cumberland and Westmorland Record Office,
Leconfield MSS. Box 110

(c) *The Succession*

The Act of Settlement of 1701 made statutory provision for a Protestant succession after Anne's death but offered no guarantee that this provision would be carried out. This was one reason why the succession remained an active party issue right up to 1714. Later other factors came into play, notably the Tory election triumph of 1710 and the loss of confidence by Hanover in the good intentions of the Oxford ministry during the years 1711-14.

The Union of England and Scotland (1707), which on the English side was mainly the handiwork of the Whigs, remedied one serious deficiency in the provisions of 1701, the fact that they had not applied north of the Border. But the most significant reinforcement of the Act of Settlement in England was achieved by the Regency Act of 1706. This measure, designed to prevent a collapse of authority in the dangerous interval between Anne's decease and the arrival of the Hanoverian heir, was the reply of the Whig Junto to a factious motion by the High Tory opposition in the Lords in November 1705, whereby it was proposed to invite over the Dowager Electress Sophia to England. The 'Hanover motion' was made not out of affection for the Electoral house but out of a desire to embarrass Godolphin and the Whigs to the utmost; since the Queen was known to be as violently opposed to sending such an invitation as Sophia was anxious to receive one. The Whigs were certainly embarrassed, but it was the Tory cause that suffered most in the long run. The Tories were devastatingly mocked by Lord Wharton for their sham 'conversion' to zealous Hanoverianism, and they cut an even sorrier figure by their subsequent tactics in obstructing the progress of the Regency bill (1).

Prevarications of this kind gave the Whigs a splendid chance to raise the bogy of Jacobitism against their opponents at the next General Election. In pamphlets like *The Advice to the Electors of Great Britain* (2) the Tories were accused of encouraging the Pretender's attempt to invade Scotland in the spring of 1708, though as far as the English were concerned there was no substance in the accusations. Such warnings to the electorate would have been more appropriate in 1710 than in 1708. For in 1710 large numbers of known or suspected Jacobites were elected to the House of Commons – more, perhaps, than at any time since 1690. They were not yet ready to show their hand openly in Parliament; but as the Tory party's commitment to Hanover grew weaker over the next three and a half years (especially after the quarrel between the Oxford ministry and the Elector over the making of peace in 1711), so the Jacobite cause attracted growing sympathy.

The Whigs made a great effort to put the succession issue squarely before the public from the summer of 1713 onwards, for they realised that it was the most vulnerable chink in their opponents' armour. They succeeded so well that in 1713-14 Tory members in both Houses split into recognised groups of Jacobites and pro-Hanoverians (3). Over many questions – for example, the demand by the Hanoverian envoy, Baron Schütz, for a writ summoning the Electoral Prince to the House of Lords (3, **ii**) – the two groups were utterly at odds; and in April 1714 the Hanoverian Tories joined with the Whigs against the government and the rest of their own party in the great votes on the Court motion that the succession was not in danger under the Queen's administration (4). Although these motions were carried, they did much to destroy the cohesion of the Oxford ministry. Its members, successful neither in convincing Hanover of their loyalty nor in persuading the Pretender to change his religion, had therefore no common strategy agreed on to meet the final crisis when it came at the end of July and the beginning of August. And thus the Whigs, whose unity remained absolute as long as the succession issue dominated all others, were able to take control of the situation and to welcome the unexpectedly peaceful accession of George I with a great sense of deliverance (5).

1 The 'Hanover Motion' and the Regency Bill, 1705-6

(i) Burnet's account of proceedings in the Lords after the failure of the Tory motion to invite the Electress Sophia to England, November 1705

The Lords were now engaged to go on in the debate for a regency. It was opened by the Lord Wharton in a manner that charmed the whole House. He had not been present at the former debate, but he said he was much delighted with what he had heard concerning it. He said he had ever looked on the securing a Protestant succession to the crown as that which secured all our happiness. He had heard the Queen recommend from the Throne union and agreement to all her subjects, with a great emotion in his own mind. It was now evident there was a divinity about her when she spoke; the cause was certainly supernatural, for we saw the miracle that was wrought by it. Now all were for the Protestant succession. It had not always been so. He rejoiced in their conversion, and confessed it was a miracle. He would not, he could not, he ought not to suspect the sincerity of those who moved for inviting the next successor over. Yet he could not hinder himself from remembering what had passed in a course of many years, and how men had argued, voted and protested all that while. This confirmed his opinion that a miracle was now wrought; and that might oblige some to show their change by an excess of zeal, which he could not but commend, though he did not fully agree to it.

After this preamble he opened the proposition for the regency, in all the branches of it: that regents should be empowered to act in the name of the successor till he should send over orders; that besides those whom the Parliament should name, the next successor should send over a nomination sealed up, and to be opened when that accident should happen, of persons who should act in the same capacity with those who should be named by Parliament. So the motion, being thus digested, was agreed to by all the Whigs, and a bill was ordered to be brought in pursuant to these propositions.

But upon the debate on the heads of the bill, it did appear that the conversion which the Lord Wharton had so pleasantly magnified was not so entire as he seemed to suppose: there was some cause given to doubt of the miracle; for when a security that was real and visible was thus offered, those who made the other motion [the 'Hanover motion'] flew off from it. They pretended that it was because they could not go off from their first motion. But they were told that the immediate successor might, indeed, during her life continue in England; yet it was not to be supposed that her son the Elector could be always absent from his own dominions, and throw off all care of them and of the concerns of the Empire, in which he bore so great a share. If he should go over for ever so short a time, the accident might happen in which it was certainly necessary to provide such an expedient as was now offered. This laid them open to much censure, but men engaged in parties are not easily put out of countenance.

... The Tories made some opposition to every branch of the act ... I never knew anything in the management of the Tories by which they suffered more in their reputation than by this. They hoped that the motion for the invitation would have cleared them of all suspicions of inclinations towards the Prince of Wales, and would have reconciled the body of the nation to them and turned them against all who should oppose it. But the progress of the matter produced a contrary effect. The management was so ill disguised that it was visible they intended only to provoke the Queen by it, hoping that the provocation might go so far that in the sequel all their designs might be brought about, though by a method that seemed quite contrary to them and destructive of them.

Own Time, v, 234-9

(ii) Lord Somers to the Elector of Hanover, 12 April 1706

It might have a strange appearance that they, who by a long and steady series of acting had shown themselves, beyond a possibility of dispute, the assertors of the succession in the person of her Electoral Highness, the Princess Sophia, should in the least hesitate to agree to a proposition that it was necessary to have the next presumptive heir to the crown to reside in England. But I beg leave to suggest to your Electoral Highness's consideration that if this had been allowed for a rule, it might possibly, in a little time, have pressed very inconvenient upon your Electoral Highness. It was not to be imagined you would leave dominions where you were sovereign to reside in England, before you were our king; and yet there would have been an inconveniency in rejecting an invitation of that nature, when the kingdom had before declared such a residence to be necessary.

But the manner of making this proposal was, above all other things,

1 THE 'HANOVER MOTION' AND THE REGENCY BILL, 1705-6

the strongest objection to it. The speech with which it was introduced [Lord Haversham's] is in print, and so cannot be misrepresented. The turn of it was to show, first, that we could go on no farther with the Dutch (which was, in effect, to say, we must make peace); and next, to say the Queen's administration was hardly sufficient to help us in peace at home, unless the next heir came over. The Queen was present at this discourse, and no one can judge so well as your E.H. whether this was a compliment proper to engage her Majesty to enter willingly into the invitation; and if it had been assented to with reluctance, whether it might not have given rise to unkindnesses that might in the end have proved very fatal.

They who were afraid of entering into such an invitation (especially coming as it did, from those who never till then showed any concern for the Protestant succession) thought it proper to lay hold of that favourable conjuncture to push in for those solid provisions which were evidently wanting, and which we hope are brought to effect by the [Regency] Act.

James Macpherson, *Original Papers containing the Secret History of Great Britain* (1775), ii, 34-5

2 The Pretender's Invasion Attempt and the General Election of 1708

... Since therefore it is plain that these two parties [Tories and Whigs] are not the least changed from what they always were, I come now to the great enquiry, whether of them is more likely to have invited over the Pretender, or to have given him reason to depend upon their interest and assistance. And in order to clear this point, I will take a short view of their several principles and practices.

The true principle of the Tories is to profess Passive Obedience and Non-Resistance; to set up an establishment opposite to liberty, void of property, and destructive of all the ends of human society; ... and in short to make a government as absolute and lawless as is possible. Accordingly, most of those gentlemen opposed the late King's coming to the crown; and when that question was carried against them, much was to be done before their consciences could be brought into a condition to own his government. The distinction of king *de facto* and *de jure* was revived, in order to make the oaths go down with them, and many made no scruple to profess that they took them in that sense, or with some other secret distinction or mental reservation...; and when the Abjuration [oath] was imposed, several that had taken the other oaths in order to save their taxes peremptorily refused this, so careful has this party been not to make their case desperate with the Pretender, not their reconciliation impracticable. Not to mention their public rejoicings, which have been often too notorious when any ill news has arrived of our misfortunes either by sea or land.

The true principle of the Whigs is to maintain the religion, liberty and property of their country; ... to keep the monarchy within its just bounds, and to secure it with laws from tyranny at home, and with forces given by Parliament from the danger of a foreign power; to reverence and esteem good Church men, yet tolerate dissenters; and in a word, to keep our excellent constitution as it now stands, between the two extremes of arbitrary power and a commonwealth. Accordingly these men in the Convention Parliament, after great difficulties and disputes, settled the crown upon the present establishment, and have since taken effectual care for securing the succession.... They have broke all measures with the Pretender, have been constantly unanimous against his interest, and have upon every occasion with one consent acknowledged her Majesty to be their rightful and lawful Queen.

> Arthur Mainwaring and the Duchess of Marlborough, *Advice to the Electors of Great Britain; occasioned by the Intended Invasion from France* (Edinburgh, 1708), p. 2

3 The Tory Split on the Succession, 1713-14: Hanover Tories and Jacobites

(i) A Jacobite M.P. reviews the state of Parties in the session of 1714

There was in this Parliament the Court party, consisting of such as adhered, some to the Lord Oxford, and some to the Lord Bolingbroke; and though these joined in most votes, it was well enough known that their two leaders were endeavouring to supplant each other and would soon break out into an open rupture. There were likewise the true

3 THE TORY SPLIT ON THE SUCCESSION, 1713-14

blue Whigs, who resolved to oppose the Court in all things they pretended to or aimed at, and endeavoured by all means to blacken their reputation, by crying down the peace, setting forth the danger of Popery and exposing the bad administration of the public revenues. The discontented Tories made a third party. These, however, pretending to be true Churchmen, did join with the other Tories in all things which related to the interest of the Church, but in all other matters they concurred with the Whigs in opposition to the ministry, and particularly affected an extraordinary zeal for the Hanoverian succession, distinguishing themselves by the name of Hanoverian Tories, at whose head Sir Thomas Hanmer, the Speaker, appeared. The ministry, however, whilst assisted by the other Tories, who in opposition to the Hanoverian may be called the Jacobite Tories, carried all points by a great majority.

... Strange principles directed, and unaccountable notions influenced, these odd animals called the Hanoverian Tories. And the truth of it is, their actions were so inconsistent with their professions, they lost their characters and become the jest of all mankind. They pretended to reconcile the doctrine of non-resistance and passive obedience with the principles on which the Revolution was founded and by which the deposing of kings was justified. They maintained that the succession to the crown was indefeasible and hereditary, and that the settlement thereof on the family of Hanover was no infringement. They professed a great zeal for the Church and the laws and constitution of old England, and yet they broke in upon them daily and prosecuted those measures which they themselves foresaw would terminate in the utter destruction of them. These are plain paradoxes, and nothing but downright infatuation could move men of sense and figure in the world to act and think so inconsistently.

Commentaries of George Lockhart of Carnwath, Esq. (The Lockhart Papers, ed. A. Aufrere, 1817, pp. 442-3, 475-6)

(ii) The Tories and the Electoral Prince of Hanover, 1714

Anon to Baron Bothmar, 14 May 1714

The Pretender's faction acknowledge that if the Prince comes over their whole scheme is overturned; and there is no lie which they do not invent to destroy the hopes of the Prince's coming, quoting letters from Hanover which tell that Monsieur Schütz has been disavowed and very ill received, and that it is certain the Elector will not send the Prince to England. Mr. Secretary Bromley, in particular, spoke in this manner, which has thrown the Pretender's faction into transports of joy, and the friends of Hanover, both Whigs and Tories, into the utmost despair...

I beg your Excellency to make this known to his Electoral Highness. Consider what advantage the Pretender's friends will draw from it, and whether, your friends being rebuffed and disgusted, it will not be an easy matter for your enemies to carry any bill they please in Parliament infringing the acts governing the succession... The boldness of these people goes so far that Sir John Pakington, in a *Club* or meeting of more than 80 Tories, proposed that the Parliament should order the black box to be opened; so they call the sealed instruments of the Electress appointing regents in the event of the Queen's death. But the affair was dropped.

This, and other things still worse, will be revived at this time if the Prince does not come...

Brit. Mus. Stowe MSS. 227, fo. 44

4 The Commons' Debate on the Danger to the Succession, 1714

Sir John Perceval to Philip Perceval, 17 April 1714

I had the good fortune last Thursday to get into the House of Commons and hear a debate of very great consequence. The Court side were resolved to vote the succession not in danger under her Majesty's administration, which they carried accordingly as you have seen by the Votes. But a great body of the Tories agreed with the Whigs to oppose it. They sat from 12 [noon] till 9 at night, and at last the courtiers got the victory by only 48: so that they told me, as Pyrrhus said, many such victories will ruin us. All my Lord Anglesey's interest, with the Duke of Argyll's, the Earl of Abingdon's and Sir Tho. Hanmer's voted against the question. The last is universally admired for his speech that day; only courtiers resent it. The ministry were not spared, the Peace was pulled to pieces, and it was often urged how unreasonable it was to bring the Queen's name to shelter an evil ministry.

Sir Tho. Hanmer said he hoped the House would never descend so low as by this vote to screen a ministry, and that it was giving the House reason to suspect them that their friends should press it in such a manner; that he knew many honest and sensible men who were afraid the succession was in danger, and he was sure the authority of the House of Commons would not convince them otherwise; that for his part, he would not say it was, or was not, but that if there was danger this vote, if credited without doors, would but increase that danger, by lulling the people asleep at a time when they should look about them. He spoke about 10 minutes, as I judge, and his appearance gave a great life to those who opposed the question. Sir H[enry] Bunbury spoke also against it, and so did Ward, the Queen's Council, Sir Arthur Kay, and several others from whom it was not expected. Four-score and odd Tories divided against the Court, and the House was the fullest that ever was known in the memory of any man. 256 against 208.

Add. MSS. 47027, pp. 192-3

5 A Whig Paean on the Peaceful Accession of George I

Bishop Burnet to [Lady Russell?], n.d. [August 1714]

I... take occasion to vent my heart to your Ladyship. What reason have we all to rejoice in God who has now saved us by a train of wonders. We were, God knows, upon the point of at least confusions, if not of utter ruin, and are now delivered and rendered as safe as any human constitution can be. A person lately come from Paris says the consternation was great, and that they were cursing our ministers, who had made them believe that thing[s] were of themselves working so for the Pretender that the game was sure, though no foreign assistance were given. But with what trouble must we think of the brave men of Barcelona, who probaby must be cut off at last.[1]

I congratulate both with L[ady] Galway and your Ladyship this

[1] The reference is to the abandonment in the peace settlement of 1713-14 of the Catalans, the chief supporters of the Habsburg cause in Spain.

glorious turn of affairs. God make us all thankful for it and help us to make the use for which God has sent us these extraordinary blessings.

Chatsworth MSS. Devonshire Family Papers, 36.8

(d) *Religion*

Before the Revolution the Whigs had favoured tolerant treatment of Protestant dissenters, who had been firm supporters of their Exclusion policy (1679-81), while the Tories had consistently championed the privileges of the Anglican Church and supported its harsh attitude towards nonconformity. The Toleration Act (1689) was a qualified victory for Whiggery and brought substantial relief to Dissent, from religious though not from civil disabilities. But it did not remove religion, nor even the issue of toleration, from the arenas of party conflict. After a few years of relative quiescence, religious problems asserted themselves anew to become the most disturbing ideological factor in politics.

In the late 1690's there arose from the High Tories, both clerical and lay, the cry of 'the Church in danger'. For twenty years at least it became the favourite battle-cry of the Tory party, in pulpit and pamphlet, in Parliament and polling-place. Some of the alarm which Tories claimed to feel was genuine. William III's government was lax in its interpretation of religious legislation. After Queen Mary's death in 1694 moderate or 'Low Church' divines came increasingly into favour and the episcopate grew more Whiggish. Most important, the lapsing of the Licensing Act in 1695 encouraged an outpouring of writings critical of, or downright hostile to, the basic tenets of orthodox Anglican theology [cf. **J.2**]. The High Tories thought it no coincidence that this development occurred at a time of Whig political supremacy, and they campaigned for the recall of Convocation in the hope of closing the floodgates (**1, i**). When the Whigs began to regain their grip on the government in 1705 their opponents tried to persuade both Houses of Parliament to vote the Church in danger under the present administration. They failed. But the Whig persecution of Sacheverell four years later gave them a new and Heaven-sent opportunity. From the first day on which the Doctor's sermons were brought to the notice of the Commons (**1, ii**) they raised a storm over the safety of the Church of England which raged with unprecedented violence for nearly twelve months and did much to sweep away the Whig ministry.

M (d) RELIGION   115

The dissenting churches gained in strength after 1689 at the expense of the Established Church, and more and more of their adherents became prominent in the nation's life. High Tories were convinced that the main reason for this advance was their success in breaching the two main statutory defences of exclusive Anglicanism, the Act of Uniformity and the Test Act. In particular they denounced the practice of 'occasional conformity' by dissenters for the sake of office and deplored the progress being made by the dissenting academies. In the years of their greatest political influence (1702-4 and 1711-14) they attempted to close both these avenues of advance by means of new legislation, and in so doing convinced the nonconformists and the Whigs that they were bent on subverting the Toleration itself (**2, iii; 3**).

The outcry against the occasional conformists began with Edwin's case in 1697 (**2, i**), but it was another five years before it produced major party warfare in Parliament. Encouraged by Anne's accession to the throne, and inflamed from the pulpit (**2, ii**), the extreme Tories introduced their first and most malevolent Occasional Conformity bill in November 1702 (**2, iii**). Undeterred by its eventual failure, they followed it with two further bills, one in each of the next two sessions. The Whigs consistently opposed them (**R.2**). The Tories, on the other hand, became at each stage more divided over the prudence of such a measure in wartime, until eventually a majority of them refused to follow their leaders' advice to force it past the Lords by means of a 'tack' to a money bill.

A good deal of political manoeuvring, as well as a conflict of religious principle, characterised the struggle over the first three Occasional Conformity bills (**2, iv**). The High Tories were concerned not only to defend the Church but to attack the dissenting vote. Throughout our period this was an important factor in Whig electoral success, in corporation boroughs especially, as the Wilton case showed in 1702, (**4, i**), but also in some other constituencies (**4, ii, iii**).

A milder version of the Occasional Conformity bill eventually passed into law in 1711 during the life of the Oxford ministry. This time the Whigs, to earn the political support of the bill's sponsor, Lord Nottingham, acquiesced in it – a fact which caused them embarrassment later and partly explains why they delayed the act's repeal until 1719. Before then, however, they had regained their reputation with the dissenters by their staunch opposition to the Schism bill of 1714, the measure whereby Bolingbroke and Atterbury planned to destroy Dissent at its roots in the field of education (**3**). It is worth remembering, none the less, that many Whigs were against removing outright the civil disabilities of Protestant nonconformists by the abolition of the sacramental test, while the vast majority opposed a relaxation of penal laws against Roman Catholics. The Whigs were a tolerant party; but they were not the Party of Toleration, in the widest sense.

1 'The Church in Danger', 1697-1710

(i) The Recall of Convocation demanded, 1697

[Francis Atterbury and others], *A Letter to a Convocation Man, concerning the Rights, Powers and Privileges of That Body* (London, 1697)

In plain English, then, I think that if ever there was need of a Convocation, since Christianity was established in this kingdom, there is need of one now: when such an open looseness in men's principles and practices and such a settled contempt of religion and the priesthood have prevailed everywhere; when heresies of all kinds, when scepticism, Deism and atheism itself overrun us like a deluge; when the Mosaic History has by men of your own order been cunningly undermined and exposed, under pretence of explaining it; when the Trinity has been as openly denied by some as the Unity of the Godhead sophistically opposed by others; when all mysteries in religion have been decried as impositions on men's understandings, and nothing is admitted as an Article of Faith but what we can fully and perfectly comprehend; nay, when the power of the Magistrate and of the Church is struck at, and the indifference of all religions is endeavoured to be established by pleas for the justice and necessity of an universal Toleration, even against the sense of the whole Legislature. At such a time, and in such an age, you and I, Sir, and all men that wish well to the interests of religion and the State, cannot but think that there is great need of a Convocation.

pp. 2-3

(ii) Dr. Sacheverell Vindicated, December 1709

... a complaint was, on the 13th of December, made in the House of Commons of two printed books: the one entitled *The Communication of Sin; A Sermon preached at the Assizes held at Derby, August 15, 1709*, by Doctor Henry Sacheverell, and the other entitled *The Perils of False*

1 'THE CHURCH IN DANGER', 1697-1710

thren both in Church and State; set forth in a Sermon preached before the Right Honourable the Lord Mayor, Aldermen and Citizens of London at the Cathedral Church of St. Paul's, on the 5th of November, 1709, preached also by the said Dr. Henry Sacheverell; ... Which books were delivered in at the Table ...

... John Dolben, Esq. [Whig M.P. for Liskeard] made the first motion against the two sermons, and was seconded by Spencer Cowper, Esq. [Whig M.P. for Beeralston]. But they were opposed by several [Tory] gentlemen, who said they did not perceive there was anything in the sermons malicious, scandalous or seditious; nor reflecting on her Majesty and government, the late happy Revolution and the Protestant Succession. What concerned both Houses of Parliament was supposed to be the vote passed four and five years before about the Church being in danger. And as to that it was affirmed the Church was then in danger, was still in danger, and it was to be feared would always be in danger; not from her Majesty's administration, but from Papists on the one hand and fanatics on the other; from these her professed enemies, and from false brethren. It was owned there were some warm expressions in the sermon preached at St. Paul's; and no wonder that a true son of the Church of England should express himself with some warmth and vehemence against the liberties that were taken, and with impunity, to revile the Church, her doctrines and ministers, to blaspheme the name of God, and to insult and treat with contempt everything that is sacred.

A Compleat History of the Whole Proceedings of the Parliament of Great Britain against Dr. Henry Sacheverell (London, 1710), pp. 3-5

2 Occasional Conformity, 1696-1704

(i) The Scandalous Behaviour of Sir Humphrey Edwin, November 1697

R. Yard's Newsletter to Sir J. Williamson, Whitehall, 11 November 1697

The present Lord Mayor, Sir Humphrey Edwin, has for two Sundays together gone to Mead's meeting-house in London, attended by the sword-bearer with the city sword and the other officers. This has given great offence, even to the most considerate dissenters, who look upon it as a very imprudent act which may do them prejudice. The court of aldermen have taken notice of it, and, after expressing their dislike thereof, have passed a vote that the city sword should not be carried to any meeting or conventicle.

Calendar of State Papers Domestic. 1697 (1927), p. 467

(ii) Henry Sacheverell's Oxford Sermon, June 1702

... Now what I have proved of religion in general, and its tendency to promote the happiness and welfare of government, will appear much more evident in the particular application of it to ourselves of the Church of England, as it stands upon a legal foundation, established and distinguished from all that confused swarm of sectarists that gather about its body, not to partake of its communion but to disturb its peace, and presume to shelter themselves under its character, not to support and maintain, but more effectually to undermine and destroy it: a distinction that ought carefully to be guarded and observed by every true son of our Church, inasmuch as it excludes out of it all those false and perfidious members, who under the pretence and hypocritical disguise of 'charity' and 'moderation' would have taken down its fence, and removed its land-mark, to make way for all men of a free and unbounded persuasion to enter ... In order to which pious design its Test[1] must be abolished, all its worst enemies tolerated, nay its very articles expounded out of their true sense and wrested from their genuine meaning ... to comply with those very persons they were on purpose framed to keep out of its sacred and inviolable communion. But these shuffling, treacherous Latitudinarians ought to be stigmatised, and treated equally as dangerous enemies to the government as well as Church. For the royal throne and the divine altar seem so inseparably joined and united in each other's interests that the one can only be maintained by the true principles and establishment of the other ...

If therefore we have any concern for our religion, any true allegiance for our sovereign, or regard to the safety and honour of our country, we must watch against these crafty, faithless and insidious persons who can creep to our altars, and partake of our sacraments, that they may be qualified [for office], more secretly and powerfully to undermine us: ... such a religious piece of political hypocrisy as even no heathen government would have endured. And for the relief of which destructive injury, though she has so long laboured in vain, yet, blessed be God, there is now a person on the throne who so justly weighs the interest of Church and State as to remove so false an engine, that visibly overturns both.

[1] The sacramental test imposed on office holders in 1673.

In a word, let us be true to ourselves and our profession, ... and let us scorn to trim, waver and double with the opinions and interests of these halters betwixt God and Baal, but let us steadily adhere to the good, old staunch principles of our Church, and fear not. Though she is troubled on every side, she shall never be distressed; though she is perplexed, yet she shall not be in despair; though she be persecuted, she shall not be forsaken; though cast down, shall not be destroyed; neither shall the Gates of Hell be ever able to prevail against her.

The Political Union. A Discourse shewing the Dependance of Government on Religion (London, 1702), pp. 48-50, 61-2

(iii) Bishop Burnet on the Introduction of the 1st Bill against Occasional Conformity, November 1702

When those matters were settled, a bill was brought in by the Tories against Occasional Conformity, which produced great and long debates. By this bill, all those who took the sacrament and Test (which by the act passed in the year 1673 was made necessary to those who held offices of trust or were magistrates in corporations,[1] but was only to be taken once by them), and did after that go to the meetings of dissenters, or any meeting for religious worship that was not according to the liturgy or practice of the Church of England, where five persons were present more than the family, were disabled from holding their employments, and were to be fined in an hundred pounds, and in five pounds a day for every day in which they continued to act in their employments after their having been at any such meeting ... But whereas the Act of the Test only included the magistrates in corporations, all the inferior officers or freemen in corporations, who were found to have some interest in the elections, were now comprehended within this bill.

... Some thought the bill was of no consequence, and that if it should pass into a law it would be of no effect; but that the occasional conformists would become constant ones. Others thought that this was such a breaking in upon the Toleration as would undermine it, and that it would have a great effect on corporations; as indeed the intent of it was believed to be the modelling elections, and by consequence of the House of Commons.

[1] The Anglican qualification for municipal office holders was necessitated not by the Test Act but by the Corporation Act of 1661.

On behalf of the bill, it was said, the design of the Test Act was that all in office should continue in the communion of the Church; that coming only once to the sacrament for an office, and going afterwards to the meetings of dissenters, was both an eluding the intent of the law and a profanation of the sacrament which gave great scandal, and was abhorred by the better sort of dissenters. Those who were against the bill said the nation had been quiet ever since the Toleration; the dissenters had lost more ground and strength by it than the Church; the nation was now engaged in a great war; it seemed therefore unreasonable to raise animosities at home in matters of religion at such a time; and to encourage a tribe of informers, who were the worst sort of men. The fines were excessive, higher than any laid on Papists by law, and ... men would be for ever exposed to the malice of a bold swearer or wicked servant ...

All who pleaded for the bill did in words declare for the continuance of the Toleration. Yet the sharpness with which they treated the dissenters in all their speeches showed as if they designed their extirpation.

Own Time, v, 49-51

(iv) The Politics of the Occasional Conformity Bills, 1702-4

[Simon Clement], *Faults on Both Sides* (1710)

The mystery of this project was to raise the spirits of the Tory party, to create in the Queen an opinion of their formidable strength, and by degrees to model the corporations, weed out the dissenters, and at length to disable them in their electing members of Parliament; and their design was still more evident when in the third session they attempted to tack it to the Land Tax bill, that if by that compulsion they should get it passed, or if the Lords (as they had formerly declared) would rather reject a money bill than admit of any tack, the Queen might be overawed by their power and necessitated to take them into her ministry. But here they quite lost themselves and broke their reputation for ever since, and the bigotted party-men had herein a convincing instance how much their leaders use them as tools to work their own ends; for several of the most considerable men of that side having been taken off by the ministers, and gratified with good places, they left their party in the lurch, and voted against the Tack. And thus this noisy, mischief-making, party-driving, good-for-nothing bill came to be utterly lost.

2nd edn. pp. 26-7

3 The Schism Bill, 1714

The Humble Supplication of Certain of Her Majesty's faithful and Peaceable Subjects called Protestant Dissenters ... in relation to the Bill to prevent Schism (London, 1714):

It cannot but be a grief to all your Majesty's good subjects, who wish to see the whole nation united in affection to your Majesty and in zeal for the public safety, to find that to the present unhappy breaches, which too much agitate the minds of your subjects, and which break in upon the peace of societies, neighbourhood, and even of families, about state affairs, which few rightly understand, should be added the revived rancour and animosity which so long, and with so many evil effects, distracted this nation for fifty years before the Revolution upon differences in religion; all which the charity and forbearance of the Church of England, and the satisfaction which the dissenters reaped in an uninterrupted toleration, had happily laid asleep, and which began, on both sides, to be forgotten among us ...

We acknowledge, Madam, that taking away the schools and academies of the dissenters is not an immediate depriving us of the Toleration; though it abridges us of those appendices of liberty which we enjoyed as consequences of the Toleration, as aforesaid ... But we humbly represent to your Majesty that these things cannot but fill us with just apprehensions that farther hardships may be prepared and designed for us; and that those who can be so unjust to us as to insinuate that we are dangerous to your Majesty's interest, unworthy of your royal favour ... will not fail, as far as possible, upon all occasions, to incense your Majesty against us, and to prepossess your Majesty so far in our prejudice as to make other and farther hardships and restraints upon us to seem necessary; and at last, to bring upon us a repeal even of the Toleration [Act] itself, and a return of all the former violences of persecution, under which we and our immediate progenitors have so deeply suffered already.

We farther represent to your Majesty that as it may be true that we may ... send our children for education and instruction to foreign parts, whereby the succession of our ministers may be preserved, yet that this confirms our apprehensions, as aforesaid, that our enemies will not rest here, but are resolved if possible to push on their designs against us to our entire ruin ...; since otherwise the easiness of our bringing up young ministers abroad, whereby ... the end of the present design will be defeated, should be a forcible reason against their proceeding against us in this manner, as being a thing perfectly ineffectual, and not capable of answering what is proposed by it (viz.) of putting an end to what they call the Schism.

pp. 30-34

4 The Dissenting Vote

(i) WILTON, 1701-2

Mr. Bromley (according to Order) reported from the Committee of Privileges and Elections the matter, as it appeared to them, touching the elections for the borough of Wilton in the county of Wilts...

That the right of election was agreed to be in the Mayor and burgesses. That upon the poll there were, for Sir John Hawles, 37; for Mr. Bodington, 37; for Mr. Gauntlet 24.

That the petitioner's [Gauntlet's] counsel argued that the Mayor and burgesses constituted the Corporation, and did all corporate acts; and therefore, according to the Act of 13 Car. II for the well governing and regulating of Corporations, they ought to have received the Sacrament according to the rites of the Church of England within one year before they are elected burgesses. The counsel said they should, on this head, object to several, viz. to 20 that had voted for Sir John Hawles and to 21 that had voted for Mr. Bodington; and that they had long since delivered a list of their names to the sitting members. That of these, 19 had been made burgesses between the 1st of September 1701 and the 25th of June 1702.

... Thomas Danet said, he was at the former election of Parliament men, and that as soon as it was over, the Mayor and burgesses returned to the Council-house, where the Mayor spoke to this effect: that Sir Henry Ashurst and Mr. Gauntlet had then carried the election; but, before another election, he would make so many new burgesses, there should be no occasion for the old to attend. William Mare, another, testified he had heard the Mayor say that he would make none burgesses that were not Dissenters from the Dam's Teat; for if they chose Churchmen, they would be always against them.

... And that the Committee came to these resolutions: *Resolved*, that it is the opinion of this Committee that the election of any person to be

4 THE DISSENTING VOTE 123

a burgess of Wilton, in the county of Wilts, who has not taken the Sacrament of the Lord's Supper according to the rites of the Church of England within one year before such election, is a void election ...

Commons' Journals, xiv, 49: 28 Nov. 1702

(ii) COCKERMOUTH, 1710

'A true copy of a letter from the [leading dissenters of the] borough of Cockermouth to his Grace the Duke of Somerset, dated 14 Sep 1710'

May it please your Grace,

Though we can't but acknowledge you are justly entitled, by your bounty to us on many occasions, to our votes and interest for one representative for this borough, yet you must allow us at this juncture to prefer our own choice of members to serve in Parliament to all considerations whatsoever, and to acquaint your Grace that unless you will be pleased to recommend to us again Major General Stanhope we cannot promise to give you a vote for any other person of less moderation and zeal for our service.

His Excellency the E[arl] of W[harton], Lord Lieutenant of Ireland (according to his interest, goodness and zeal for us and our cause) recommends Mr. Lechmere for the other representative, who did with the Major General also nobly distinguish himself in the late trial of the Church, in managing the impeachment of the C[ommons] against that *malignant, seditious, discontented, hotheaded, unedified preacher of sedition and rebellion, that insignificant, inconsiderable tool of a party, Sacheverell*.

And though her present Majesty does not seem to have her countenance towards such choice members as we endeavour to set up, because forsooth they seem to call her hereditary title and prerogative in question, and though some perhaps may also think it unmannerly in us to bestir ourselves on the behalf of men of such opinions and principles, yet the cause of God['s] religion and our pure (but poor, distressed church) calls upon us at this juncture to exert our utmost zeal and hearty endeavours to have good and godly members in the next Parliament, as well as we had in the last, that our Christian liberty may be in no danger of being cramped or invaded by the immoderate High-flying Church men. It would be a sin in us, or any of our profession in Great Britain, now to sit still and be idle when we have due hopes of such glorious managers. Our friends in Whitehaven join with us in this humble representation, in which if we succeed we would not despond of carrying on and perfecting a Godly and thorough reformation both in Church and State.

Cumberland and Westmorland Record Office,
Leconfield MSS. D/Lec 110

(iii) SURREY, 1714-15

G. Whitehead to the Earl of Nottingham, 22 November 1714

Understanding by our friend Daniel Quare that thou desirest our recommendation for thy kinsman, the Lord Guernsey's son, to be chosen a knight of the shire for Surrey, whereupon we are in a strait and at a stand, because we understand he was for promoting the Schism bill (now an Act), which if we should do we cannot answer it either to our f[rien]ds in the government or at home, unless the young man can assure our friends that he is now of a better judgement than to do any such thing tending to impair or destroy our just liberties or properties, either as men or Christians (which the said bill tends to). Though for thy sake and his father's also we would go a great way to serve you, but pray excuse us in this, if thy kinsman cannot assure our friends as aforesaid.

in haste { P.S. note: we know not how to do anything against Sir Richard Onslow's interest.

Chatsworth MSS. Finch-Halifax Papers, box 3, item 128

(e) *Manifestos, Instructions and Addresses*

The practice of instructing members of Parliament by 'Advices' from their constituents was revived at the end of 1701 after having lapsed since the period of the Exclusion crisis. As the Buckinghamshire Advice illustrates (1), it offered the Whigs, especially, an admirable vehicle by which to parade their views on the great issues of the moment. The five documents which follow all reflect the importance which the parties attached to issues in wooing the electorate. Three of them date from the spring and autumn of 1710 and show the Tories defining their own position and impugning that of their opponents on a wide range of the questions we have been surveying, as well as on certain associated problems like the naturalisation of foreign Protestants. At the same time they illustrate the different priorities of the constituent elements of the Tory party, ranging from the High Toryism of the borough of Westbury and the more moderate and 'Hanoverian' Toryism of the candidates for London in 1710 to the responsible, Harleyite creed of George Granville (2). There follows a rare example of a candidate's address to his constituents *after* election (3). Finally we are reminded how the unscrupulous propagandist of the day, by seizing on the views of extreme minorities on a variety of questions and presenting them as the party norm, could easily produce a grotesquely false picture of his opponents' principles and programme for the benefit of the more gullible electors (4).

1 Instructions to Whig Members, 1701

Aylesbury, Dec. 11

The Advice of the County of Bucks to their knights of the shire.

We, the gentlemen and freeholders of the county of Bucks who have now made choice of you to represent us, do depend on you that you will seriously consider that the trust we have reposed in you is of the highest consequence to us and our posterity, and as you value the blessing of Almighty God and the future goodwill of your county, we do exhort, charge and require that you fail not to support the King with the most effective and most equal supplies;

That you endeavour by all methods to restore and keep the credit of the nation;

That you heartily concur in such alliances as the King has or shall make for pulling down the exorbitant power of France, and enable him to make good the same;

That you consider of all ways for maintaining the succession as by law now established;

That you discover, if possible, who they are among us that have any regard, friendship or allegiance to the new Pretender which the French would impose upon us, that such may fall under your just indignation...

And that in time of danger, especially, you avoid all such differences, disputes and animosities, as so lately had like to have undone us;[1]

[1] The reference is to the attempted impeachment of the Whig leaders by the Tories in the previous session.

taking due care at all times to enquire into and punish all real crimes and mismanagements in public affairs.

These things, and whatsoever else that will appear to you to be necessary for the defence and preservation of our religion and liberty, and the liberties of all Europe, we heartily recommend to you; and we doubt not of your best endeavours, and of the blessing of Heaven on so just and righteous a cause.

The Electors' Right Asserted (London, 1701), p. 14

2 Professions of the Tory Faith, 1710

(i) The Humble Address of the Borough of Westbury to the Queen, 14 April 1710

We are deeply sensible that the many and signal victories which your arms have obtained abroad, and the settled peace and tranquillity which your subjects have enjoyed at home, have been owing first to the goodness of God, and next, under that, to the felicity of your Majesty's government. As we earnestly desire the continuance of these blessings, so we do, from the bottom of our hearts, lament the growth of atheism and irreligion, which may justly provoke God to withdraw his mercies from us, and the revival of those rebellious principles by which this Church and State have once been laid desolate... [We] shall, to our utmost power, oppose these schismatical and republican spirits, whom nothing can content but the extirpation of episcopacy out of the Church and the subversion of that hereditary monarchy which is so happily established in the State.

We have better learned the duty of our inferior stations than to intermeddle in the weighty affairs of government. But when your Majesty shall judge it expedient to summon a new Parliament, we promise to choose such representatives as shall be unsuspected of having any inclination to change; gentlemen of known affection to your Majesty's person, title and prerogative, and at the same time careful to preserve the just rights and liberties of the subject; determined by a principle to maintain the doctrine, worship and discipline of the Church of England, and by a true Christian moderation to continue that indulgence which our laws have granted to consciences truly scrupulous; willing to contribute to the carrying on of the war, whilst absolutely necessary, and ready to concur in such measures as may most tend to procure a speedy, safe and lasting peace.

A Collection of the Addresses ... presented to the Queen since the Impeachment of ... Sacheverell (London, 1711), Part I, p. 17

(ii) George Granville to [the High Sheriff?] of Cornwall, London, 29 September 1710

The enclosed letter from my Lord Rochester his Lordship desires may be communicated to the gentlemen with you. I wish her Majesty's service would have permitted me to have presented it to you with my own hand, but I hope you will have goodness enough to consider the necessity of affairs that has kept me.

If it shall be judged proper for the service of the county to recommend me for one of their representatives, I think myself obliged beforehand to make this solemn protestation, that I may be accepted or rejected according as my principles are approved, which are

To support monarchy and the Church for which so many of our ancestors have sacrificed their lives and fortunes together to establish the Protestant succession beyond any possibility of dispute.

To restore the credit of the nation, which her Majesty has so happily retrieved by the late exercise of her royal authority.

To carry on the war against France with such vigour and such intentions as may produce a safe, honourable and speedy peace.

And lastly to serve the county [of] Cornwall in particular, in every respect that can any way regard to its advantage, with the utmost power and interest that I can any way collect.

I desire only to be tried in these principles, I having nothing to value myself upon but having my veins so full of Cornish blood as to have the honour of being related perhaps to every one of the gentlemen to whom you may have an opportunity at this time to communicate my sentiments ...

Carew Pole MSS. (Buller Papers), BO/23/63

(iii) Election Address of the Tory Candidates for the City of London, October 1710

London, October 9, 1710

Sir,

This day comes on the election of members for this city, in which your vote and poll is desired for the four worthy citizens undernamed to be your representatives in the ensuing Parliament; viz.

Sir William Withers } Knights, and Aldermen
Sir Richard Hoare }

Sir Geo. Newland } Commoners
John Cass, Esq }

who are qualified for that high trust: by their dutiful submission and respect to the Queen's most Excellent Majesty, in all her lawful commands; by their affection to the Protestant succession settled by Parliament in the illustrious House of Hanover; by their unalterable desire to live under a Limited Monarchy, without invading the just prerogatives of the Crown, or betraying the rights of the subject; by their zeal for the Established Church, without any tincture of Popery or bigotry; by their tender regard to the indulgence granted to consciences truly scrupulous ... and who, by an easy access to their persons, will be ready to carry any complaint or grief of the people to Parliament for redress; and being independent of the Court, their debates, votes, and resolutions will be free; and themselves without fears for the old ministry, or how their behaviour will be taken by the new; and who are for cultivating a good understanding with our Protestant neighbours, without complimenting away our commerce, or inviting them to intermeddle in the affairs of our government, or to send over the scum of their countries to make ourselves, who already abound in poor, yet poorer[1]; and lastly, who have not entertained such vast hopes of profit from the continuation of the war as to remain wholly unconcerned for a general peace; neither are they interested so far by their large shares in the Bank as to be careless of the growth or decay of our national trade, on which depends the life of this great City, and the strength and defence of the kingdom.

The Supplement No. 427, 6-9 Oct. 1710

---

[1] A reflection of Tory hostility to the Whig Naturalization Act of 1709 and the invitation to the 'poor Palatines'.

3 Robert Walpole's Address to the Electors of King's Lynn, 1713

Gentlemen –

I cannot but think myself entirely obliged to you for the favours bestowed on me this day. But more especially I think myself particularly bound to offer you my most hearty thanks for your kindness in electing me after that malicious prosecution of me,[1] inasmuch as you were pleased to stand by me, because you dare to be honest in the very worst of times; and this act of yours will render this corporation famous to the later posterity. The late Parliament (from whom no good could be expected, nor no good came) addressed her Majesty to use her interest with all foreign states to remove the Pretender from their dominions, but this hath been so well complied with that he is at present removed as near us as the power of France can place him. Gentlemen – her Majesty was pleased to tell us (as you all know) a year past that Dunkirk should be demolished, but not one stone is removed, and the completion of that work is deferred till Christmas, and whether it will then be demolished we have no certainty. And as to the terms of peace, I dare be bold to affirm that had the King of France beaten us, as we have done him, he would have been so modest as to have given us better terms than we have gained after all our glorious victories. Gentlemen – we have some reason to think that the ensuing Parliament will tread in the same steps with the former, but assure yourselves we will struggle hard for our religion and liberty.

Hist. MSS. Comm. *Portland MSS.* v, 333

4 Tory Manifesto for the 1715 Election

These things it may be of use to weigh, . . . that this is the most critical juncture ever happened; that if the country errs in their choice of representatives now, it will probably be never more in their power to do themselves justice; and that the sale of a man's vote, even for a hundred pound, a price frequently offered, is a wretched bargain, because it is selling it for ever.

Upon the whole, I am far from arrogating to our own party all the

---

[1] The reference is to his expulsion from the House of Commons and imprisonment in the Tower by the Tories in 1712.

good sense and virtue of the nation; but, compare the bulk of each side together, and you will find the Whigs positively bad, the churchmen negatively good. According to which computation I have cast up the account, for the benefit of those who may be at too great a distance from the fountain of affairs to know the true state of them. The following bill of their several deserts is, I think, very exact.

The Merits of the Church-Party.	*The Merits of the Whigs.*
I	I
No new war, no new taxes.	A new war, six shillings in the pound, a general excise, and a poll-tax.
II	II
No attempt against the Church.	A general and unlimited comprehension, without common-prayer book or bishops.
III	III
No repeal of the conditions upon which the crown was settled upon the King.	The repeal of the Act of Limitation of the Crown, etc.
IV	IV
No foreigners in employment.	An equal distribution of places between Turks, Germans, and infidels.
V	V
No standing army.	An augmentation of troops for the better suppressing of mobs and riots.
VI	VI
No long parliament.	The repeal of the Triennial Act.
VII	VII
No restraint of the liberty of the press.	An Act to prohibit all libels in favour of the Church or Churchmen, and to enable all freethinkers to write against God and the Christian religion.

VIII	VIII
No insulting the memory of the Queen.	An encouragement to all men to speak ill of the Queen and her friends.
Total	*Total*
No alteration of the constitution in Church and State.	An entire and thorough revolution.

Utrum horum mavis accipe

Choose which you please

> Francis Atterbury, 'English Advice to the Freeholders of England' (1714), *Somers' Tracts* (1815), xiii, 541

INTERESTS

Since the nineteenth century, when Marx's work created considerable interest in the social foundations of politics, historians have sought to verify or refute his contention that political conflict was the expression of class struggle. During our period society was divided politically into two classes, the ruling elite, which was a tiny minority, and the ruled. However much antagonism there might have been between these two classes during the period of the Civil War and Interregnum, however much there was to be from the reign of George III onwards, there is little sign of it during the late seventeenth and early eighteenth centuries. Though the privileges of the ruling classes increased after 1689, while the vast majority of Englishmen became in many ways more and more oppressed, this process produced no radical movement akin to the Levellers or even to the Yorkshire Association.

That is not to say that there were no social tensions beneath the party struggle of the years 1694-1716. Though the issues which divided Whig from Tory had a valid existence independent of any cleavage in society they were given a sharper edge by the real or imagined grievances of individual social interests within the ruling elite itself. For this political elite was not a homogeneous social class, but included a fair cross-section of educated society – landowners, businessmen and professional men. The landowning section, composed of the aristocracy and gentry, was overwhelmingly superior in numbers. Among the businessmen were financiers and merchants, but only a few industrialists – shipbuilders and mineowners for example – since society had not yet become industrialised. The professional men consisted of the clergy, the lawyers, army and navy officers, and occupants of posts at all levels of the administration.

There were, of course, rivalries *within* these groups. The bulk of the gentry had good cause to envy the prosperity and political preeminence of the substantial squires and noblemen. The business world was very far from being united. Between 1698 and 1709, for instance, there were even two East India Companies engaged in cut-throat competition. In Convocation the inferior clergy kept up a running fight with the bishops from 1701 to 1717. These tensions, as we have already observed in the case of the clergy (**H**) were worked out in the party struggle. Most country gentlemen were Tories, while peers and bigger landowners were often Whigs, as in Kent (**5**). Macaulay observed that 'nowhere was the conflict between Whigs and Tories sharper than in the City of London; and the influence of the City of London was felt to the remotest corner of the realm'.[1] This was certainly the case in the General Election of January 1701, when the New East India Company looked to Whig candidates, and the Old Company to Tory candidates, to sponsor their interests in Parliament (**1**).

Of far more importance, however, to the substance of conflict in the years 1694-1716 was the animosity *between* social groups and interests. Country gentlemen were resentful of the fact that their predominant place in the political elite was being challenged by merchants and soldiers (**2, i**). They retaliated by passing the Property Qualifications Act of 1711, which insisted upon the possession of real estate by members of parliament (**2, ii**). Though the Act was passed in a predominantly Tory Parliament it had the approval of some at least of the Whig

[1] Lord Macaulay, *The History of England* (ed. T. F. Henderson, 1907), p. 756.

country gentlemen, as the observations of Lord Molesworth demonstrate (6). The conflict of interests was not at all times a party controversy.

The most explosive clash of all, however, that between the landed and the moneyed interests, became a mighty party cause. The nature of this conflict is frequently misunderstood because it is seen as one between all landowners on the one hand and all businessmen on the other. The 'landed interest' of contemporary parlance included not landowners at large but only those who lived solely on their income from rents. The 'moneyed interest' was an even more restricted part of the community. It was composed of those who lent money to the government, together with such men as factors and stockbrokers who, in Bolingbroke's words, 'added nothing to the common stock'. By no means all businessmen had surplus capital to advance to the State. On the other hand some substantial landowners had, and these ought properly to be included in the moneyed rather than in the landed interest.

War finance drove a wedge between these two interests. The land tax was levied at the rate of four shillings in the pound between 1692 and 1712, except for the short break between the Peace of Ryswick and the outbreak of the War of the Spanish Succession. Though its incidence was not uniform, where it was efficiently assessed it really did mean a 20% levy on rents, which was the highest rate of direct taxation until the twentieth century. Government creditors, by contrast, could obtain handsome returns on their investments. The Act of 1694 which set up the Bank of England to facilitate the raising of public loans guaranteed 8% interest on the first £1,000,000 raised. This led to a clash between the two interests, which soon merged into the party conflict when the Tories espoused the 'landed interest' while the 'moneyed interest' was championed by the Whigs. As early as the summer of 1694 Lord Sunderland was apprehensive of the Tory leaders' determination to 'break the Bank' in the next session of Parliament.[1] In William's reign the Tories even tried to set up a Land Bank to offset the Whiggish corporation in the City, but this failed lamentably [see **A.4**]. By Anne's reign the power of the Bank, and with it that of the whole 'moneyed interest', had grown enormously (3), until in 1710 four Bank Directors presumed to warn the Queen not to dismiss her Whig ministers (4). This unprecedented act scandalised the landed gentry, and as long as the war lasted the gulf between the two interests was unbridgeable.

[1] N.U.L. Portland (Bentinck) MSS. PwA. 1237: Sunderland to Portland, 6 July 1694.

1 The Two East India Companies and the General Election of 1701

Upon the view of the House [of Commons] it appeared very evidently, that the Tories were a great majority. Yet they, to make the matter sure, resolved to clear the House of a great many that were engaged in another interest. Reports were brought to them of elections that had been scandalously purchased by some who were concerned in the new East India Company. Instead of drinking and entertainments, by which elections were formerly managed, now a most scandalous practice was brought in of buying votes, with so little decency that the electors engaged themselves by subscription to choose a blank person, before they were trusted with the name of their candidate. The old East India Company had driven a course of corruption within doors with so little shame that the new Company intended to follow their example, but with this difference, that, whereas the former had bought the persons who were elected, they resolved to buy elections. Sir Edward Seymour [the leader of the High Tories in the House of Commons], who had dealt in this corruption his whole lifetime, and whom the old Company was said to have bought before, at a very high price, brought before the House of Commons the discovery of some of the practices of the new Company. The examining into these took up many days. In conclusion, the matter was so well proved that several elections were declared void; and some of the persons so chosen, were for some time kept in prison; after that, they were expelled the House. In these proceedings, great partiality appeared; for when, in some cases, corruption was proved clearly against some of the Tory party, and but doubtfully against some of the contrary side, that which was voted corruption in the latter, was called the giving alms in those of the former sort.

Own Time, iv, 475-6

2 Gentry versus Army and City, 1708-10

(i) James Lowther to William Gilpin, 12 February 1708

There is mighty clamours against having so many officers of the army in the House, and they will certainly be routed sooner or later, which would make elections easy enough in our country [Cumberland]. And the people ought to be apprised of the unreasonableness of having three [M.P.'s] in six officers of the army. There never was more need for men of estates to be chosen, when officers of the army and merchants of London are jostling the landed men everywhere out of their elections.

Carlisle Record Office, Lonsdale MSS.

(ii) Peter Wentworth to Lord Raby, 21 December 1710

I was yesterday in the gallery to hear the debate of the Commons upon the commitment of the Place bill, but just as I got in they called out for the question, and the House divided . . . When they came into the House again I got in, and heard Mr. St. John move to have a day appointed for the commitment of the Qualifying bill . . . Mr. St. John's speech was pretty remarkable, for in setting out how necessary this bill was to be enacted he gave some touches upon the late management, as that we might see a time when the moneyed men might bid fair to keep out of that House all the landed men, and he had heard of Societies of them that jointed stocks to bring in members, and such a thing might be an administration within an administration, a juncto; and these moneyed men might arise to such a pitch of assurance as to oppose the Crown and advise in matters that did not belong to them . . .

The Wentworth Papers (ed. J. J. Cartwright, 1883), p. 167

3 The Grievances of the Landed Interest, 1709

Henry St. John to Lord Orrery, 9 July 1709

Your Lordship hints at . . . the spirit of our gentlemen, and what is to be expected from it. Alas, my Lord, nothing. Examine a little this chain of causes. We have now been twenty years engaged in the two most expensive wars that Europe ever saw. The whole burden of this charge has lain upon the landed interest during the whole time. The men of estates have, generally speaking, neither served in the fleets nor armies, nor meddled in the public funds and management of the treasure.

A new interest has been created out of their fortunes, and a sort of property which was not known twenty years ago is now increased to be almost equal to the terra firma of our island. The consequence of all

[this] is, that the landed men are become poor and dispirited. They either abandon all thoughts of the public, turn arrant farmers, and improve the estates they have left; or else they seek to repair their shattered fortunes by listing at Court, or under the heads of parties. In the mean while those men are become their masters, who formerly would with joy have been their servants. To judge therefore rightly of what turn our domestic affairs are in any respect likely to take, we must for the future only consider what the temper of the Court, and of the Bank, is.

Bodleian Library, MS. Eng. Misc. e. 180, fos. 4-5 [copy]

4 The Bank intervenes in Politics, 1710

[Robert Harley] to Arthur Moore, 19 June 1710

About twelve days since Sir Gilbert Heathcote [the Governor of the Bank] wrote to a great Lord earnestly desiring that he and some others might speak with the Duke of Devon[shire] and the Lord Privy Seal [the Duke of Newcastle]. In a day or two after a meeting was fixed, at which were present the Duke of Devonshire, Duke of Newcastle, Sir G. Heathcote, Sir William Scawen, Mr. Eyles, and Mr. Nathaniel Gould. Sir G. Heathcote was the spokesman; he in very strong and earnest terms pressed the two dukes to go to the Queen, and in their name to dissuade her from making any change in the ministry; particularly if Lord Sunderland [Secretary of State] was put out dismal consequences would follow; that he had nothing to do with, nor any dependance on, the ministers, but that he for the public good could not forbear telling his opinion, and that all credit would be gone, stock fall, and the Bank of England be ruined, which included the ruin of the nation, with many other tragical expressions.

It was the beginning of last week before this was reported to the Queen, after which the same four gentlemen were introduced to tell their own story themselves to the Queen. The Secretary by that time being removed, Sir Gilbert Heathcote thought fit to alter his speech and to speak to her Majesty of the danger of altering her ministers, and dissolving the Parliament.

This is a matter of a very extraordinary nature, that private gentlemen (for it cannot be conceived for their own sakes that the Bank deputed them), that private persons they should have the presumption to take upon them to direct the sovereign. If this be so let us swear allegiance to these four men and give them a right to our passive obedience without reserve.

Hist. MSS. Comm. *Portland MSS.* iv, 545

5 Social and Party Divisions in Kent, 1713

[Rev.] John Johnson to [Dr. Charlett], Cranbrook (Kent), 5 September 1713

We carried it for Sir Edw[ard] Knatchbull and Mr. Hart by above 650 voices against the two noblemen [Hon. Edward Watson and Hon. Mildmay Fane], which is a deadly blow to the Whiggish interest in this county. This time 3 years [ago] there were ten Whigs elected in this county and but 8 Church-men: now we have 13 Church-men, and but 5 Whigs. I pray God that we may have equal success in other counties: and the truth is I think the settlement and future peace of the nation do entirely depend upon a good majority of honest Church-men in the L[ower] House . . .

I can't but observe to you, that though we have now twice together carried it in this county for the Church by a very great majority, as likewise in our two cities, yet all our temporal peers, except Thanet and Sussex (for Winchelsea does not concern himself with the public), and the very great majority of our richest gentlemen are Whigs: insomuch that at a general rendezvous of both parties at last Assizes, when both sides were to nominate their candidates, there were at least 60 noblemen and gentlemen on the Whiggish side, very few more than 30 on ours.

Bodleian Library, MS. Ballard 15, fo. 107

6 The Country Whigs and Landed Qualification

Robert Molesworth's Reflections on Politics [c. 1711]

An old [Country] Whig is for choosing such sort of representatives to serve in Parliament, as have estates in the kingdom; and those not fleeting ones, which may be sent beyond sea by Bills of Exchange by every packet-boat, but fixed and permanent. To which end, every merchant, banker, or other monied man, who is ambitious of serving his country as a senator, should have also a competent, visible land estate, as a pledge to his electors that he intends to abide by them, and has the same interest with theirs in the public taxes, gains and losses. I have heard and weighed the arguments of those who, in opposition to this, urged the unfitness of such whose lands were engaged in debts and mortgages to serve in Parliament, in comparison with the monied man who had no land: but those arguments never convinced me.

The Memoirs and Secret Negotiations of John Ker of Kersland (Part iii, London, 1726), p. 205

O

PLACE AND POWER

Parties were brought into existence by the clash of opinions on the great issues of the day and the conflict of interests, but their ultimate goal was the tenure of political power so that they could transform their ideas into policies, or protect their component interests by legislation. The struggle to seize or retain places at Court, and indeed throughout the administration, thus occupied a good deal of the energies of active politicians. In William's reign the Whigs fought to retain their hold on the ministry, and to expel their rivals (**1, i**), while St. John recalled that in 1710 the immediate aim of many Tories was to obtain complete control over places from top to bottom (**4, i**).

To some politicians the pursuit or the preservation of place became an end in itself. St. John, who on a matter of principle had resigned the Secretaryship-at-War in 1708 and left the ministry along with his friends, Harley and Harcourt (**S.6**), expressed his disgust at the naked greed for the emoluments of office which so many Tories displayed in 1711 (**4, ii**). When William Bromley stood for the Speakership of the House of Commons against a Court candidate in 1705 his supporters brought great pressure to bear on members of whom it was rightly suspected that, though as Tories they ought to support him, as placemen they would vote against him (**2**).

Yet it cannot be too strongly emphasised that to most men actively

O PLACE AND POWER 139

engaged in the political struggle from 1694-1716, at least at the higher levels, place was a means to an end: it was not enough without power. That is why in 1698 the Whigs objected to serving with Tories because a 'pieced business' would thwart their measures. They wanted party government, with the full support of the King, not the mixed ministries which William preferred (**I**, **ii**; also **S.5**, **10**). Lord Wharton's faith in the Whig concept of party government stood up most remarkably to the temptations of a place in 1708, when his financial affairs were extremely precarious (**3**). Even St. John, when a cyincal and disillusioned exile in 1717, conceded that the Tories of 1710 sought power not only to reward their friends but to conserve what in their view comprised 'the public good of the nation' (**4**, **i**).

1 Parties and Places, 1697-8

(i) The Duke of Shrewsbury to Lord Somers, 14 April 1697

... his Majesty said, some alterations were necessary in the customs and excise ... and upon that occasion declared, that several had so behaved themselves this session that if no punishment were made, no government could be expected for the future, and said, this must not be extended partially to one kind of men, but some should be displaced of different denominations. In general, I agreed with this; but submitted that a distinction was reasonable to be made between persons who had done wrong only once through ignorance, and those who, in the whole course of business, had continually opposed. This argument met with so cold a reception that I think it is not hard to guess what was meant by that speech, though I think if it be intended against Sir Walter Young and Mr. Clarke, we are obliged (I am sure I think myself so) to stand by them. This sort of discourse naturally brought on that of my Lord President [the High Tory Duke of Leeds], etc., and I was surprised to find how easy the King was in parting with him, and his consequences. He said, the whole family of the Berties were against him ...

Hardwicke State Papers (ed. P. Yorke, 1778), ii, 431

(ii) Lord Somers to the Duke of Shrewsbury, 25 October 1698

At present he [the King] is without anything which has the appearance of a ministry; the plain consequence of which is, that everybody (seeing the little credit those have who serve him) is in a manner invited to ruin or expose them.

If one could have his wish, it is very hard to find men to supply even present vacancies; especially considering the King's prejudices to some, and his fondness for others, and the power which my Lord Sunderland still has. There is nothing to support the Whigs but the difficulty of his piecing with the other party; and the almost impossibility of finding a set of Tories who will unite.

So that, in the end, I conclude it will be a pieced business, which will fall asunder immediately ...

Ibid, pp. 435-6

2 A Party Appeal to a Placeman's Conscience, 1705

[Lord Digby] to Edward Nicholas, 10 October 1705

Br[omley] is gone up I believe, and has been told by several he may depend upon your vote. I hope he will not be deceived, for your sake. For this I find will be made the test of men's integrity: and your opinion is so well known, and if your vote should not go with it, the world will ascribe it to something that is not very honourable. I know temptations will be laid in your way, but give me leave to say there can be no temptation for a man in your circumstances; nor can there be a price for a man's integrity in any condition. This I know you are sufficiently sensible of, and therefore I may perhaps be impertinent in saying it. But what passed between us at S[haftesbu]ry upon this subject has made me a little uneasy, and given me some apprehensions lest a wrong notion of gratitude or some other false argument should mislead you in a thing of so much concern both to yourself and your country. For I do think a great deal more depends upon this than the having a Sp[eake]r our friend. All the world sees now which way things are tending (and particularly by this last step) and there is nothing so likely to stop this cancer as a majority of the H[ouse] of C[ommons] appearing early against it.

Brit. Mus. Egerton MSS. 2540, fo. 136

3 Honest Tom Wharton refuses a Bribe, 1708

Arthur Mainwaring to the Duchess of Marlborough, July 1708

... Yesterday ... I was in the morning with Lord Wharton ... who said he had just before had a long conference with the Duke of Somerset which I will make as short as I can. His Grace, with the air of a great minister, told him what endeavours had been used to bring in Lord Somers, which had proved ineffectual; but that it was not out of any aversion which the Queen had to the [Whig] party in general, but something that was personal to that lord, upon account of his having disobliged the Prince [Consort]; that if one Whig could not be received, he had reason to think another might; that nobody could have greater talents and better pretensions to any employment than his Lordship, and that he might command his service and good offices with the Queen, for whatever could be acceptable to him. To which my Lord answered, after some preambles about his own unworthiness and insufficiency, that he thought making distinctions among men of the same principles and interest was not the way to do the nation's business; that if he had ever been of any service, it was chiefly owing to the assistance of his friends, from whom he would never divide, nor could do it without making himself quite inconsiderable; that he thought it would be much more for the service and honour of his Grace and the ministers to put themselves at the head of the whole party, which would make them strong, and carry them through all their present difficulties; than to think of dividing them again, which would only increase their troubles of last year ...

Blenheim MSS. E.25

4 St. John on the Motives of the Tories, 1710-11

(i) I am afraid that we came to court in the same dispositions as all parties have done; that the principal spring of our actions was to have the government of the state in our hands; that our principal views were the conservation of this power, great employments to ourselves, and great opportunities of rewarding those who had helped to raise us, and of hurting those who stood in opposition to us. It is, however, true, that with these considerations of private and party interest there were others intermingled, which had for their object the public good of the nation, at least what we took to be such.

We looked on the political principles which had generally prevailed in our government from the Revolution in one thousand six hundred and eighty-eight, to be destructive of our true interest, to have mingled us too much in the affairs of the Continent, to tend to the impoverishing our people, and to the loosening the bands of our constitution in Church and State. We supposed the Tory party to be the bulk of the landed interest, and to have no contrary influence blended into its composition. We supposed the Whigs to be the remains of a party, formed against the ill designs of the Court under King Charles the second, nursed up into strength and applied to contrary uses by King William the third, and yet still so weak as to lean for support on the Presbyterians and other sectaries, on the Bank and the other corporations, on the Dutch and the other allies. From hence we judged it to follow that they had been forced, and must continue so, to render the national interest subservient to the interest of those who lent them an additional strength, without which they could never be the prevalent party. The view, therefore, of those amongst us who thought in this manner, was to improve the Queen's favour to break the body of the Whigs, to render their supports useless to them, and to fill the employments of the kingdom, down to the meanest, with Tories.

Henry St. John, Lord Viscount Bolingbroke,
A Letter to Sir William Windham (1753), pp. 19-22

(ii) Henry St. John to Lord Orrery, 12 June 1711

Many changes have been made at the rising of the Parliament, which was this day prorogued to the 10th of July; and although they are such as ought to satisfy our friends, yet the number of the discontented must always exceed that of the contented, as the number of pretenders does that of employments. I confess to you, my Lord, that it made me melancholy to observe the eagerness with which places were solicited for; and though interest has at all times been the principal spring of action, yet I never saw men so openly claim their hire, or offer themselves to sale. You see the effects of frequent Parliaments, and of long wars, of departing from our old constitution, and from our true interest.

Letters and Correspondence of Henry St. John, Lord Viscount Bolingbroke (ed. G. Parke, 1798), i, 245-6

P

COURT AND COUNTRY

Long before the words 'Tory' and 'Whig' became current in the Exclusion crisis the terms 'Court' and 'Country' had been used to describe political alignments, being very roughly equivalent to the more modern expressions 'government' and 'opposition'. This older terminology survived the Revolution. Indeed in the early nineties it seemed more appropriate to describe the realities of politics than the use of party labels. William's first ministries were composed of men of all shades of political opinion, and their supporters formed a 'Court' party which to one disillusioned observer had allowed the fruits of the Revolution to wither on the vine (**I, i**).

The concept of politics as a conflict between 'Court' and 'Country' rather than one between Whig and Tory was prevalent even in the years 1694 to 1698, when the 'Court' was much more closely identified with the Whigs than it had been earlier. This was in large measure due to the fact that the Whig party had originated as an opposition party. Many Whigs were unable to adjust to this new situation in which some of their leaders had accepted office, and were now dependent on the support of men who had places and pensions, some of whom had previously sided with the Tories. These leaders were regarded as apostates from true Whiggery by many of their erstwhile supporters, whose sense of betrayal underlines the extract from *The Danger of Mercenary Parliaments* (**I, ii**: cf. **A.5**; **M**(b).**3**).

The Court party appeared formidably strong to its critics, but they grossly exaggerated ministerial control over the Commons. Indeed after the peace of Ryswick in 1697 that control slipped out of the hands of the Junto into those of the leaders of the Country party. In the first two sessions after the peace the Court was unable to resist Country demands for the reduction of the armed forces. William wanted to keep some 30,000 men in arms, and the Court party did what it could to oblige him, but in the session 1697-8, as John Methuen informed a correspondent, 'the country gentlemen [were] all generally against the army any more than about ten or twelve thousand'.[1] Having reduced

[1] Blenheim MSS. Sunderland Letterbooks vol. 3: Methuen to anon, 8 Jan. 1698.

the army to this level, after the General Election of 1698 they brought it down yet further to 7,000 (**2, i, ii**).

The Country party's aim of restricting the power of the executive extended much further than the reduction of the army. In many ways its greatest triumph was the inclusion in the Act of Settlement in 1701 of numerous restrictions on the prerogatives of the future Hanoverian kings. [Cf. C.3, where it is implied that these were solely Tory-inspired]

But already by 1701 the political conditions which had perpetuated the old Court/Country terminology, and which had created the new Court and Country parties, were changing. In the years 1700-2 there was a further polarisation of political parties towards the extremes of Whig and Tory (**C**). One result of this was that by Anne's reign the Country party of the nineties had split up into its component parts: Country Whigs and Country Tories. Backbenchers in both parties continued the Country tradition, but they no longer formed an identifiable party. Even the term 'Country party', so frequently encountered in William's reign, was hardly ever used in Anne's.

The Country tradition was continued mainly in attacks on the influence of the Crown. One of the greatest concessions wrung from the Court in the Act of Settlement was a clause providing for the expulsion from the House of Commons of all placemen on the death of Anne. Many Country members, impatient for that event, introduced measures known as place bills or self-denial bills to expel at least some officials while the Queen was still alive. Anne's ministers, on the other hand, took the first opportunity to modify the effect of the sweeping provision of 1701. This occurred in the session of 1705-6, when the passage of the Regency bill through parliament was used by the government to repeal the obnoxious clause. The Country members resisted this attempt. At first, on the initiative of the Country Tories, they continued to insist on the complete disqualification of all placemen. Later, at the suggestion of the Country Whigs, they proposed instead a clause limiting the number of placemen in the House of Commons to forty. Those Country Whigs who sponsored this proposal were known as the 'Whimsicals', and the clause itself as the 'Whimsical clause'. It was eventually defeated, but not before the ministers had been obliged to substitute a more restrictive place clause in the Regency bill for the one they had initially proposed.[1]

Sir John Cropley was one of the leaders of the Whimsicals (**3, i**). His patron, the third Earl of Shaftesbury, who was grandson to the leader

[1] G. S. Holmes, 'The Attack on the "Influence of the Crown", 1702-1716', *Bulletin of the Institute of Historical Research* (1966), xxxix, 47-68.

of the first Whigs, had been an enthusiast for Country measures during William's reign. He had advocated the Treason Trials Act of 1696, whereby accusations of treason had to be backed up by two witnesses, and the accused was to be allowed counsel, and also a property qualifications bill, not unlike that which became law in 1711 (see **N.2, ii**). His advocacy of pure Country measures in Anne's reign gave his Whiggery a curiously old-fashioned flavour (**3, ii**). For the pattern of backbench politics was changing. However suspicious the Country Whigs or the Country Tories became of the Court they only united against it on such *ad hoc* occasions as those provided by place campaigns. They no longer formed a party on the basis of identity of interests. Rather they formed pressure groups within their own parties, such as the Whimsical Whigs of 1706, the October Club Tories of 1711 (see **D.3**) and the March Club Tories of 1712 (**4**). The activities of such pressure groups reflect, at times quite startlingly, the sophistication which party politics acquired in the exceptional conditions of the period 1694-1716.

1 The Court Party in William's Reign

(i) *A Short State of our Condition, with Relation to the present Parliament* (printed about November 1693)

... when think you shall we have a new election now, since the King has about six score members that I can reckon who are in places, and who are thereby so entirely at his devotion, that although they have mortal feuds when out of the House, though they are violently of opposite parties in their notions of government, yet they vote as lumpingly as the Lawn Sleeves [bishops], never divide when the Interest of the Family, as they call it, is concerned, that is to say when any Court-Project is on foot. The House is so officered, that by those that have places and pensions, together with their sons, brothers and kinsmen, and those who are fed with the hopes of preferment, and the too great influence these have upon some honest mistaken country gentlemen (who are possibly overfrighted with the *French*), the King can baffle any bill, quash all grievances, stifle accounts, and ratify the Articles of Limerick ...

I once thought to have affixed to this paper a list of those that are in office; which if I had, it would not only have shown how many members are bought off, but would have pointed out many amongst the number of favourites and pensioners who we expected should rather have been punished. Had we intended to have justified what we have done to after-times; had anything but personal grandeur been the real intention of him who we intended to have been, and valued himself most upon being, our Deliverer [William III]; these men must have been marked down as betrayers of their country, who are now made the chief supporters of his throne. I thought we called over the Prince of Orange to get or give us all the laws we wanted; to have made the elections of Parliament secure and frequent, trials impartial, the militia our standing force, and the navy our strength. I thought we had called him over to call ministers to account, and to have put it out of their power impunibly to abuse us hereafter . . .

I could name a certain gentleman who exactly resembles Harry Guy [Secretary to the Treasury], that the last sessions, when the House was a little out of humour, disposed of no less than sixteen thousand pounds in three days' time, for secret service. Who are in places we may find out, but God knows who have pensions; yet every man that made the least observation can remember that some who opened loudly at the beginning of the last sessions, who came up as eager as is possible for reformation, had their mouths soon stopped with Hush-money . . .

State Tracts (1706), ii, 369-71

(ii) *The Danger of Mercenary Parliaments* (1698)

Fatal experience has now more than enough convinced us that Courts have been the same in all ages, and that few persons have been found of such approved constancy and resolution as to withstand the powerful allurements and temptations which from thence have been constantly dispensed for the corrupting of men's minds, and debauching their honest principles. Such instances of the frailty of human nature may be given within these few years past, as might make a man ever ashamed of his own species, and which (were they not so open and notorious) ought out of pity to mankind to be buried in perpetual silence. Who can enough lament the wretched degeneracy of the age we live in? To see persons who were formerly noted for the most vigorous assertors of their country's liberty, who from their infancy had imbibed no other notions than what conduced to the public safety, whose principles were further improved and confirmed by the advantages of a suitable conversation, and were so far possessed with this spirit of liberty, that it sometimes transported them beyond the bounds of moderation, even to unwarrantable excesses: to see these men, I say, so infamously fall in with the arbitrary measures of the Court, and appear the most active instruments for enslaving their country, and that without any formal steps or degrees, but all in an instant, is so violent and surprising a transition from one extreme to another without passing the mean as would have confounded the imaginations of Euclid or Pyrrho ...

The necessity we have lain under of frequent meetings of Parliament during the war has taught our managers so much dexterity and address in their applications to the members of that assembly that they are now become consummate masters in that most detestable art of attaining or losing offices and preferments. And though I here name offices, yet those offices are downright bribes and pensions, since they are held precariously from the Court, and constantly taken away upon noncompliance with the Court-measures; though I am not ignorant that several considerable pensions were also laid out of the Exchequer to members of both Houses: for places could not be had for all, though they have tried all imaginable arts for dividing among themselves the considerable posts in the kingdom: for either by splitting of offices among several persons, which were formerly executed by one, or by reviving such as were sunk, or by creating others which were altogether useless and unnecessary, or by promises of preferment to those who could not presently be provided for, they had made above two hundred members absolutely dependent upon them. And what points might not such a number carry in the House, who were always ready and constantly attending with more diligence to destroy our constitution than the rest were to preserve it?; who represented not their country but themselves, and always kept together in a close and undivided phalanx, impenetrable either by shame or honour, voting always the same way, and saying always the same things, as if they were no longer voluntary agents, but so many engines merely turned about by a mechanic motion, like an organ where the great humming basses as well as the little squeaking trebles are filled but with one blast of wind from the same sound-board?

State Tracts (1706), ii, 641

2 The Country Party in William's Reign

(i) Robert Price to the Duke of Beaufort, 11 December 1697

Yesterday the Committee of the Whole House went on the King's Speech, and immediately a question was stated that all the land forces raised since the 29th of September 1680 should be paid and disbanded, by which vote it was intended the King might keep his guards and some other forces, but not by the sanction of an Act of Parliament but by connivance. Many of the country gentlemen fell off from the Court and were for the question.

The debates for the question were most that a standing army in time of peace was express against the Bill of Rights, the Act against mutineers and deserters, the vote in 1688, the two Acts in King Charles the 2nd's time for disbanding those armies, the Petition of Right and indeed against our constitution. That a standing army in time of peace was not consistent with the being of Parliament, that it put the balance of the King's side against the people, that most of the European kingdoms lost their liberties by standing armies. That the Peace carried with it a freedom from arms and taxes, or else the country had no benefit of it. That the fear of invasion could not be, since the French king is in a lower condition now than at another time he may be or else would not purchase peace at so dear a rate. That the fleet and militia with the people's affection are the kingdom's defenders, that no invasion was ever known but where the majority of the people were for it, and generally against a standing force.

Against the question it was servilely argued of the great service the King has done the kingdom, and was he not to be trusted, and the necessity of the times and want of security. That the fleet and militia were no security; the instance of the Prince of Orange's landing that neither fleet nor military did oppose. The French king was no prince to be relied on, his treaties have been often broken; that he has not evacuated all the towns; that he disbands his own forces and lists strangers; that King James has 27 regiments of Irish in pay in France. That there is no security against the disaffected at home; that they desired the army might be annual.

But after a long debate it was carried for the question by a great majority in the cry till they would not divide. It was ordered to be reported this morning, being Saturday, when the same arguments were renewed, and after 4 hours' debate it was proposed that the amendment to the question might be made, which was (excepting 12,000) when the project failed after several proposals for 16,000 men. Then it was proposed the question should be recommitted. It was carried in the negative by 185 against 148. Then the question for agreeing with the committee, which bore no debate. I hear there were extraordinary orders for to divide to find the inclination of the House, that had they divided on the principal question, they would not have had 100. The thing aimed at is to have an establishment by Act of Parliament for 12,000 . . .

Bodleian Library, MS. Carte 130, fo. 385

(ii) Robert Price to the Duke of Beaufort, 19 January 1699

Yesterday the bill for disbanding the army was read the third time, and contrary to all expectation the Court debated against the bill that the number of 7,000 were too few and that the King's Dutch guards, who served so faithfully, were to be disbanded, and that all the French refugees being 5 regiments in Ireland and though naturalised by a particular clause in this bill were made uncapable of having any command or serving in the army. Some proposed to amend the bill and make it 10,000 men instead of 7,000, others for more, others that the bill should lie on the table and should give the King a sum but name no number. The fear of an invasion, King James, the Assassination, the discontented at home, it would lessen our security, our allies would leave us, our credit and trade would be prejudiced for want of sufficient defence, and that many would draw their money out of our funds who were foreigners. These arguments were so weak that they were fully answered and after 5 hours' debate it passed by 221 against 154. Of the 154 there were 120 officers, whereof 40 military men . . .

Bodleian Library, MS. Carte 130, fo. 397

3 Country Whigs in Anne's Reign: The 'Whimsicals', 1706

(i) Sir John Cropley to the Earl of Shaftesbury, 'Feb. 1705/6'

I think our clause died gloriously, for we have obtained the greatest concession from the Crown that ever was got . . . The self-denying Act we have obtained as one article was chiefly owing to me, and the extorting it was as their heart's blood. And though I was pretty easy under this exchange, I was forced to vote against it too, and to give the preference as I justly may to our clause, in point of honour that I might be thought to have had no hand in the bargain against our clause . . .

Our squadron is the most formidable now in the House (that is excepting the 2 great ones of Tory and Court) consisting of about 30, sufficient to turn the scale. And, for all we lost the day, 'tis visible what our power is by the Court, and by the submission made to us so conquered...

I own Lord Keeper [Cowper] almost cried to me to prevail with me to quit the clause as fatal to their being, but I showed him I was too far gone and it was out of my power... I have as yet been only against them on a Whig principle and far from personal prejudice...

Public Record Office, 30/24/20/114

(ii) The Earl of Shaftesbury to Sir John Cropley, 18 February 1706

There's nothing that in the growth of liberty I dread so much as a surfeit, nothing so dangerous as being fed too high. Our Court-Patriots that have fed us hitherto with so niggardly a hand have been better nurses of us than they imagine. Had they not so long withheld the Triennial bill, the Treason bill and kept the cup by force from our mouth when we had only a faint and false craving, we had not since taken it as good nourishment and well digested into our constitution. And though there be a plain reason why such as you and I should appear for every right thing, yet there is many a one which, whilst we countenance and promote, we may tremble for. Did I not tremble, think you, for the Treason bill when there were such plots within, and for the disbanding of the army when there was such a force abroad? What think you of that refused bill which often (when ill and dying with the fatigue) I told you lay on my heart as Calais on Queen Mary's, I mean the Qualification bill? Think you that even at this hour I should not tremble if such a bill were like to pass? But the time will come when the self-denial bill shall be full and perfect, and this afterwards crown all and rivet our constitution...

But to come to my subject matter, the dead clause: Peace be with it; but in an honourable and Christian sense, good repose for a time, and soon afterwards a glorious resurrection. Good faith, there will be little solid *peace* to the Court by the death of this so dreaded monster. You have sown dragon's teeth that will come up armed. They who might have made an honourable composition and pinned us down to half a hundred pensioners (a dreadful deadweight in our Representative) will I am confident be by degrees driven out of every post and station in that sacred part of our Constitution...

Public Record Office, 30/24/22/2

4 Country Tories in Anne's Reign: The March Club, 1712

L'Hermitage to the States-General, London, 1 April 1712 (transl.)

The March Club met yesterday, and it is said that there were over fifty present. They have left out all those who have places or pensions, or who are suspected of having them, and particularly the commissioners for examining the public accounts, considering them to be more the devotees of the Court than the others. Mr. [George] Pitt, who is an M.P. for the county of Hampshire, was placed at their head. He is said to be very wealthy, with a rent roll of more than £10-12,000, and most of the others also are among the richest men in the House... All the Club's members were in the October Club... They left it because a minister of state [Henry St. John] joined it and came to be elected President of it, and they do not wish to be governed by the Court... They are confident that their number will grow greatly because in their Club there are no Whigs.

Add. MSS. 17677 FFF, fos. 138-9

PART IV *The Arenas of Conflict*

Q

THE CONSTITUENCIES

During this period there were 513 members of Parliament for England and Wales, who were returned from 269 constituencies. Of the 245 English constituencies two, London and Weymouth, returned four members, five were single member boroughs, while the rest sent two representatives to Westminster.

The key to party organisation in these constituencies lay in the workings of electoral interests. Interest in this sense was an elusive word which could vary in meaning. To *have* an interest in a constituency could mean anything from having the right to vote there, or being able to influence men who had, to having outright nomination to one seat and sometimes to two. To *make* an interest involved combining the efforts of those who had an interest behind a particular candidate. This was the work of relatively few men. The candidates themselves were expected to make interest in their constituencies. In counties they needed the active co-operation of leading landowners, including usually peers as well as gentry. In most boroughs, too, there was a variety of interests to be marshalled – local territorial magnates, members of the Corporation, business and professional men. Only a few boroughs were at the disposal of patrons during this period. Individual interests combined to form a party organisation, so that in most constituencies there were distinct Tory and Whig interests.

In Dorset and Wiltshire the third Earl of Shaftesbury was prominent in the Whig interest. He was very active in the General Election of December 1701, and in Wiltshire claimed to have had a hand in capturing eight seats from the Tories (2). Sir Charles Shuckburgh co-ordinated the efforts of Tories in three counties in 1702 (3) – in all cases meeting success. In Aylesbury there was a strong combination of interests on both sides in 1695, the Tory cause being managed by the Marquess of Carmarthen and the Earl of Abingdon, while the Whig campaign was organised by Colonel Godfrey and the indefatigable Thomas Wharton (1).

Lord Wharton became the most renowned electoral organiser of the period. His first biographer, Sir Richard Steele, recorded that 'he was not only mindful of the county of Bucks. His care extended to those of York, Cumberland, Westmorland, Wiltshire, Oxfordshire and all places where he had estates...'[1] In 1705, according to Steele, 'my Lord Wharton exerted himself so vigorously and successfully in all parts of England, that it is said he procured the returns of above thirty members for his friends, and expended above £12,000'.[2] Though Steele almost certainly exaggerated not only the number of members returned with Wharton's help but also the amount of money which he spent, there is no reason to doubt the validity of those extracts from his *Memoirs of... Wharton*.(4) which illustrate the extraordinary combination of bonhomie and energy on which 'Honest Tom' relied to maintain his interests.

In contrast with Wharton the agent who canvassed Wensleydale and Swaledale in the summer of 1710 on behalf of Sir Arthur Kay is completely obscure. We do not even know his name. Yet his canvass is a unique picture of constituency organisation at the 'grass roots', in addition to being one of the most interesting records of local opinion to have survived from this period (5). Yorkshire, like all the English counties, was a two-member constituency. Each voter consequently possessed two votes; and not the least striking feature of the canvass is that, while one or two freeholders indicated that they would give one vote for a Tory and the other for a Whig candidate, the majority clearly intended to cast both votes on straight party lines – as indeed they did when they went to the polls in October. Lord Downe and Sir Arthur Kay, the Tory candidates, polled 6659 and 6412 votes respectively. Though Henry Boyle, at this time Secretary of State, and Conyers Darcy are both mentioned in the canvass as possible partners for Sir William Strickland, the Whig candidate, in the end he stood

[1] [R. Steele], *Memoirs of the Life of the most noble Thomas, late Marquess of Wharton* (1715), p. 31.   [2] *Ibid*, p. 38.

alone and polled only 2910 votes. These figures in themselves testify to the extent to which party conflict divided English society in this period.

1 Bribery, Browbeating and Corruption in Aylesbury, 1695

Upon the petition of [the Whig candidate] Simon Mayne, Esquire, complaining of an undue return of James Herbert, Esquire, to serve for the borough of Aylesbury the Committee have examined the merits of that election.

That, at the poll taken, there was,

For Mr. Herbert   178

For Mr. Mayne   162

But it was insisted on, by the petitioner ... that several irregularities had been practised in that election ...

That Thomas Ball, who voted for the petitioner at the last election, had promised to vote for the petitioner; but afterwards he told the said Mr. Mayne, junior, that he had received two threatening letters from Sir John Packington, and said, he was sorry he could not vote for the petitioner, but he must not ruin himself ...

And Susan Duncombe said, Edward Edwards voted for Mr. Herbert, because he had given him a black pig ...

That Richard Kempster, Friday night before the election, said he had designed [to vote] for Mr. Mayne; but Mrs. Piddrington had promised him a coat; and because her husband had not done wearing of it, and she did not give it him, he voted for Mr. Herbert ...

Edward Lewin said he saw Mr. Herbert give Mathew Little, that voted for him, some money; and he put it into his pocket without looking on it: That Mr. Herbert said nothing upon giving it; but gave it at the White Hart, the room being full of people. Mr. Mayne, junior, said Little promised to vote for the petitioner, but voted for Mr. Herbert.

1 BRIBERY, BROWBEATING AND CORRUPTION IN AYLESBURY

John Hawkes said, John Colshill confessed one of my Lord Carnarvon's servants had taken away a net from him; and that Mr. Fines, my Lord's gentleman, told him, if he would vote for Mr. Herbert, he should be paid for it: the net was valued at 15s: and that Colshill gave his vote, upon that account, for Mr. Herbert; otherwise he designed to vote for Mr. Mayne.

But Mr. Fines, being called in by the sitting member, said, he knew not of any net being taken from him, nor had offered him any money for it . . .

Ro. Holland said, Goldfinch told the people that what drink they drew for Mr. Herbert, they should be paid for . . .

Wm. Lindon said, that at the election day he went to the market hall, and was for Mr. Mayne; and that they would let in only who they thought fit; and that the Marquis of Carmarthen came up to him, and said he would make an example of him, and shook his fist at him. And Ro. Todd and John Pratt, the two constables, said, the Marquis of Carmarthen did threaten to ruin them, and fetch them up, if they did not return Mr. Herbert . . .

That for the sitting member was called,

Charles Noy: who said, that there were several persons of quality at this election, as was usual; and named the Marquis of Carmarthen, the Earl of Abington, Mr. Wharton, and Colonel Godfrey.

Wm. Church said, that Mr. Wharton, Sir Tho. Lee, and other gentlemen, being at his house the 14 Sept, the Fair-day; and Mr. Sommer fell into a passion, and asked, if all there were not friends? And if he was not, he would declare: whereupon he said Sir Tho. Lee was sure of his voice, but he would reserve his voice as to the other. Thereupon Mr. Wharton said, Church, sit down; we have no need of your voice; I bid defiance to any gentleman that shall oppose us here . . .

Resolved, that it is the opinion of this committee that James Herbert, Esquire, is duly elected a Burgess to serve in this present Parliament for the said borough of Aylesbury.

The said resolutions, being severally read a second time, were, upon the question severally put thereupon, agreed unto by the House.

Commons' Journals, xii, 417-19; 28 Jan. 1695

2 Whig Organisation in Dorset and Wiltshire, 1701

The Earl of Shaftesbury to Benjamin Furly, 29 December 1701

... It has pleased Providence to bless me with great success, for having my province (and that a very hard one) in two counties long in the hands of the most inveterate of the adverse party, I notwithstanding carried all that I attempted in both. In one of them (vizt. Wilts) which my brother and his friend represent, instead of 2 inveterate Tories, we have there mended the elections by 8, which is a difference of 16 in Parliament. And in Dorsetshire (my own county) we have gained also considerably, my friend Mr. Trenchard being in the room of a constant ill vote for the county, and my friend Sir John Cropley being also brought in by me at the place of my name, Shaftesbury, which was ever entirely in their hands since my grandfather's death, but which I have now entirely recovered, and made zealous. And as a token that the King himself is right, as we would wish, he yesterday gave me most hearty thanks for my zeal and good services on this occasion, and this before much company, which is a sufficient declaration against Sir Edward Seymour and that party, to whom my opposition was personal, and who himself in person and by his relations opposed me everywhere in the elections, though, I thank God, were everywhere defeated.

Public Record Office, 30/24/20/49

3 Tory Organisation in Gloucestershire, Northamptonshire and Warwickshire, 1702

Sir Charles Shuckburgh to Sir Justinian Isham, Shuckburgh, Sunday [July 1702]

I have sent in with Mr Brittain all my neighbours on this side, and if Captain Lucy does not force me to poll at Warwick the county I shall detach another squadron of horse to you from thence, but I can't possibly be with you this time at Northampton, having promised Jack How to go from Warwick to Gloucestershire election with him, for he stands both for town and county, for I have a list of threescore and eight votes that will not go to Gloucester unless I go with them.

Northamptonshire Archives Committee, Isham Correspondence 3022

4 Lord Wharton's Electoral Empire

(i) His Lordship having recommended two candidates to the borough of Wycombe about twenty years ago [1698?] some of the staunch Churchmen invited two of their own party to oppose them, and money was spent on both sides. A gentleman, a friend of one of the High Church candidates, was desired by him to go down to the borough with him when he went to make his interest. This gentleman told me the story, and that he was a witness of what passed when they came to Wycombe. They found my Lord Wharton was got there before them, and was going up and down the town with his friends to secure votes on their side. The gentleman with his two candidates, and a very few followers, marched on one side of the street, my Lord Wharton's candidates, and a very great company, on the other. The gentleman not being known to my Lord or the townsmen joined in with his Lordship's men to make discoveries, and was by when my Lord entering a shoemaker's shop, asked *where Dick was?* The good woman said, *her husband was gone two or three miles off with some shoes, but his Lordship need not fear him, she would keep him tight. I know that,* says my Lord, *but I want to see Dick, and drink a glass with him.* The wife was very sorry Dick was out of the way. *Well,* says his Lordship, *how does all thy children. Molly is a brave girl I warrant by this time. Yes, and thank you my Lord,* says the woman, and his Lordship continued, *Is not Jemmy breeched yet?* The gentleman crossed over to his friend on the other side of the way and cried *Even take your horse and be gone. Whoever has my Lord Wharton on his side has enough for his election.*

> R. Steele, *Memoirs of the Life of the most noble Thomas, late Marquess of Wharton* (1715), pp. 33-4

(ii) [In 1708] there was a trial [in Yorkshire] which lasted two whole days, and the Court kept sitting all the while. His Lordship, taking but one hour's rest, was present from the beginning to the end of it. As soon as the judge began to summon up the evidence to the jury, he left the Court, went into his coach and six horses, and ordered his coachman to drive him directly to Woburn [Wharton's Buckinghamshire seat] where he got about twelve at night, and rose at five next morning, set out at six for Malmesbury, where, having rode thirty miles of the way a-horseback, he arrived at night. The next day was the election for members for that borough, which he managed with that dexterity and dispatch as to carry it for both his friends, and on the morrow took coach for London. A fatigue which I could hardly have believed he was able to have gone through, as zealous and as active as he was, if I had not been informed of it by some of his retinue, who attended him all the time, but as they confessed not with the same cheerfulness and ease.

[R. Steele], *Memoirs of the life of the most noble Thomas, late Marquess of Wharton* (1715), pp. 43-4

5 Yorkshire, 1710: Canvassing Notes of a Tory Candidate's Agent

Monday, June 5.

... Mr Clark and Mr Askwith of Upsland, both Romans [Catholics] but willing to promote ...

Parson Stapylton of Watlass, a very kind and zealous friend. He will engage that he, Mr West, Mr Crossfield and Mr Purchass will bring in 3 or 400 men. He and Mr Crossfield will take care of Coverdale and Bishopdale ...

Mr Heaton of Fearby said that Sir Arthur did not ask him the last Election: and seeing him when he voted said, he might well have given him a vote, upon which Mr Heaton replied, that he might well have asked it. After some hesitation promised Sir A. his vote and all service ...

Mr Pemberton of Bedale in bed and not well – will write to Sir A.

Tuesday, June 6.

Left letters for Leonard Smelt Esq. at Kirkby Fleetham – Mr Warwick at Aiskew. Mr Samuel Atkinson of Patrick Brompton an old man and almost blind, but will send 3 sons.

The Rev. Mr Coleby, Dean of Middleham, Mr Tho. Bateman, Mr Tho. Tunstall an Attorney are very hearty friends, and all the town are Sacheverellians and value themselves mightily upon it.

Mr Edward Weterson of Middleham, a very foolish shuffling fellow, would not promise for anybody.

Mr Clayton, Rector of Wensley, has made a vow some years ago not to promise or declare himself for anybody till he comes into the Court: pretends no interest, being all thereabouts under the D[uke] of Bolton.

5 CANVASSING NOTES OF A TORY CANDIDATE'S AGENT, 1710

Mr Thornton of Redmire knows nothing of Sir A., but by the letter believes him a companion of Lord D[owne] and a good Churchman and will give him a vote (as all good Christians should do for Churchmen) but will give one for Darcy if he stands . . .

Carperby and places adjacent all the Duke of Bolton's . . .

[Castle Bolton, a seat of the Whig duke, lies very near Carperby.]

Friday, June 9.

Spoke at Greta Bridge with Mr Pinchney, Lord Rivers' Steward, who gave me good instructions how the country lay, but would not engage himself for anybody . . .

Chris^r Wilkinson Esq. of Thorpe if he stirs will serve Sir A. and Lord Downe . . . Tho. Wilkinson Esq. at Kirkbridge – abroad – I fear he's a rotten member. Mr Smith, Rector of Melsonby, was Chaplain to Mr Darcy's father, but will not be against them that will serve the Church: a gouty old fellow, but they say honest.

Mr Bruce, Rector of Middleton Tyas, a very hearty fellow and an utter enemy to Whiggism . . .

Mr Richard Burton of Scorton – a shuffler.

Mr Leonard Robinson of Scorton makes mountains of promises in our favour; he has been Clerk at 6 Elections – has an estate at Kettlewell in Craven . . . and pretends to have great interest. A fair smooth tongued fellow, but some say a great rogue.

Geo. Wright Esq. of Bolton upon Swale engaged to Strickland and Darcy. John Warthill Esq. . . . has a great respect for Sir Arthur but obliged to serve Sir Wm. Strickland . . .

Saturday, June 10, at Northallerton.

Rev. Mr Neal, the Vicar, will be very ready to serve Sir A. or any gentleman for the Church.

Edward Barstow Esq. at Hingersides obliged to serve Mr Darcy . . .

Mr Tho. Everingham of Skipton Bridge a very hearty friend. I had left a letter for him at Ripon, not thinking I should come so near him. I am told he has a good interest.

Roger Talbot Esq. at Wood End – his son gave me the answer, very ill drunk, and told me I was come to the wrong place, for they were all

Low Church men thereabouts and engaged to Strickland and he hoped Mr Boyle.

Thirsk. Mr Bell sen^r will promise nothing: an old, almost blind fellow. If I had known so before would not have troubled him.

Mr Bell jun^r. ⎫ will not engage so long beforehand.
Hy Frankland Esq. ⎭ both enemies...

Mr Tho. Stubbs of Topcliffe is engaged for Ld D[owne] and if the D[uke] of Somerset lay no contrary commands on him will serve Sir A.

Add. MSS. 24612, fos. 13-16 (transcript)

R

PARLIAMENT

Party discipline in Parliament was a matter of exhortation rather than of threats. Only the government could bring sanctions to bear on any of its supporters, by dismissing those placemen who rebelled against its measures. An opposition party could do nothing to bring aristocratic members to heel, and only a handful of M.P.'s could be cautioned with the threat of the removal of support at the next election – those returned for boroughs in the possession of patrons loyal to the party cause. The majority of members, therefore, had to be cajoled with the carrot rather than belaboured by the stick.

Nevertheless there were the equivalent of party whips, who achieved astonishing results by appealing to the faithful. During the recess party leaders conferred at country houses. The Whigs were much more assiduous in organising such meetings than the Tories, and a favourite rendezvous after 1702 for the Whig Junto was Althorp, Sunderland's seat in Northamptonshire (3). The decisions of the leaders were communicated to the rank and file by means of circular letters dispatched through a nation-wide network of contacts. The Tory preparations for an assault at the opening of a new Parliament in 1708 are particularly well documented (4).

Getting members to town when they were not obliged to attend Parliament could give the whips a headache. This did not matter so much with the House of Lords, since peers could vote by proxy. Here the important thing was to plan the collection and use of proxies carefully, since no one peer could act as proxy for more than two colleagues (**2**).

Once the members got to town organisation became somewhat easier. With the peers personal contact often sufficed (**6**). To brief backbench M.P.'s London taverns were frequently used. A black list of 1701 named 165 as 'One unanimous club of members of the late Parliament ... that met at the Vine Tavern in the Strand.' Just before the 'Tack' in 1704 150 members met at the Fountain Tavern to concert measures.[1] This seems to have been a favoured venue, for in November 1710 Lord Fermanagh wrote to his son: 'on Monday last about 200 members dined at the Fountain Tavern in the Strand, and I don't know of one Whig amongst us'.[2]

In Parliament itself party tactics were highly developed. Frequently they involved exploitation of procedure. Thus in 1697 it was only by three votes that the government supporters managed to put off protracted consideration of the King's Speech and get on with votes of supply (**1**). In 1703 the Whigs tried to get the Occasional Conformity bill rushed to the Upper House, where their friends were organised to quash it, and the Tories delayed this until what seemed a more favourable moment, by means of a procedural wrangle (**2**). The importance of procedure as a weapon in the parliamentary conflict between Whigs and Tories goes far to explain why both parties set so much store on controlling the Chair of the House of Commons (**4**; **cf. C.2**).

Not all party organisation in this period was under the direct control of the party leaders. Some of the most well-drilled manoeuvres were executed by back-bench pressure groups. One example, that of the Whimsical Whigs in the session of 1705-6 is illustrated elsewhere (see **P.3**). But without doubt the most spectacular of these groups was the Tory October Club in the session of 1710-11 (see **D.3**), which was a source of graver embarrassment to the ministry than to the Whigs, and never more so than when it sprang a surprise attack on a crucial revenue measure in March 1711 (**5**).

---

[1] Hist. MSS. Comm. *Bath MSS*, i. 64; Godolphin to Harley, 8 Nov. 1704.

[2] *Verney Letters of the Eighteenth Century* (ed. Lady Verney, 1930), i, 305; Fermanagh to Ralph Verney, 30 Nov. 1710. The figure 300 is given in the printed version of this letter, but this is an error.

1 Supply and Grievances in 1697

F. Bonet to the Elector of Brandenburg, 7 December 1697 (transl.)

Today, which the Commons had set aside to consider the King's Speech, someone in the House proposed that a supply of money should first be voted to His Majesty. But Sir Christopher Musgrave and Sir Edward Seymour and all their party opposed this, explaining that since the day was set aside for the consideration of the King's Speech they must begin with that. At this Mr. Montague replied that the House had not been held up by such formalities in recent years, and that they had always begun by voting supply to the King. To that they answered that then it had been necessary because of the war, but this no longer obtaining they ought to go back to former conventions. The aforesaid Mr. Montague replied to this that there was more need for it than ever, since all the funds were low and the King lacked money. He claimed that a major cause of this was that the credit of the Exchequer was not very great, and so they must begin with supply; the rejection of this proposal could give the public dark forebodings about this session, which would forfeit what little credit they had left. When they came to vote on this, there were found to be 157 votes for the affirmative and 154 for the negative, so in consequence they resolved to take supply into consideration tomorrow, and the King's Speech on Thursday. This is regarded as advantageous, because if they had done otherwise, they would have discovered how to delay business . . .

Add. MSS. 30,000 A, fos. 386-7

2 Party Tactics in Both Houses, 1703

C. Hatton to Lord Hatton, 9 December 1703

My neighbour Mr. Verney desires me . . . to acquaint your Lordship that by great management their House is adjourned till next Tuesday, for my Lord Whar[ton] had bragged that by proxies his party was now able to fling out the bill against occasional communion should it be now sent up. Therefore Mr. Bromley [its Tory sponsor], who was to carry up the bill, absented himself yesterday, and this day Sir Ric[har]d Onslow [Whig M.P. for Surrey] moved to have the bill carried up, which occasioned a very long debate whether according to the regular proceedings in Parliament it ought not to be carried up as soon as the person was named to carry it up. And to prevent the carrying it up immediately, upon the motion of Sir Edw[ard] Seymour the House adjourned till next Tuesday.

Add. MSS. 29576, fo. 150

3 Whig Preparations in the Summer Recess, 1707

Edmund Gibson to William Wake, Bishop of Lincoln, 29 August 1707

The Lords Sunderland, Somers, Halifax and (I think) Orford have been lately at Althorp to fix measures for the approaching Parliament, as is believed; but as for the Whig-Commons, they are shy, and will have the great ones know they are out of humour, and will have no dealings with them till they have good assurance that their services shall be better remembered than they have been. Two days ago, one of them bid me be assured that there was not yet one step made towards concerting any one thing for the next session.

Christ Church Library, Oxford, Wake MSS. Letters 17. misc. i. letter 174

4 Tory Preparations for the Opening of Parliament, 1708

(i) William Bromley to Sir Justinian Isham, Baginton (Warwickshire), 15 October 1708

Having heard that neither you nor Mr. Cartwright intend to be in town the first day of the session I take the liberty to desire you will not fail then to be there, and that if possible you'll also engage him. Our relation encourages me to be more free with you than I should be with another gentleman. I have lately seen several of our friends, and heard from more, who seem determined, if they can get a good appearance, to push for a Speaker, and hope for success from the divisions they say are of the other side. I believe gentlemen will be solicited from all parts to come up in the most pressing manner, without directly naming the reason for it, least that should alarm and unite our enemies.

Northants Archives Office, Isham Correspondence 1705

(ii) Sir Thomas Hanmer to Peter Shakerley, Mildenhall (Suffolk), 21 October 1708

I have received advice that several of our friends have discoursed together concerning the affairs which are likely to come before the next session of Parliament, and having taken the best care possible to be well informed they find reason to conclude that some matters of great moment are likely to be offered at the first opening of the session. I am desired therefore to acquaint you with this, and to request it of you that you would without fail appear the first day and also use your endeavours to prevail with all other members (friends of ours) in your neighbourhood to do the same.

You may depend upon it that care is taken to give the like notice in all other places.

(iii) Peter Shakerley to his brother George, Hulm, 27 October 1708 [enclosing a copy of the above]

The above written is a copy of a letter which I received last post, and which I desire you will immediately dispatch by a special messenger to Sir Richard Myddleton [M.P. for Denbighshire], who I hope will take effectual care to communicate it forthwith by special messengers to all the members (our friends) in Denbighshire, Flintshire, Carnarvonshire, Carmarthenshire, Merionethshire, Montgomeryshire, Anglesey and Shropshire. This day I write to our friends in Staffordshire and Warwickshire, and shall write tomorrow to those in Lancashire.

National Library of Wales, Chirk Castle MSS. E.994

5 The October Club and the Leather Duty, 1711

Peter Wentworth to [Lord Raby], 27 March [1711]

We expect now every [day] to hear you are come to the Hague. I sent you word that the P[arliament] had adjourned themselves for a week, in a compliment to their Speaker, who they found by the grief he was in for the death of his son would not be able to attend the business of the House. But 'tis believed that if Mr. Harley had not been still ill of his wound, and that they hoped by that time he might be able to come abroad, that compliment would hardly have been paid. During the recess they say the Oct[ober] Club has set their heads much together and have solicited all their friends to be sure not to fail coming to the House Monday. The Whigs were aware of this solicitation, and did not fail of giving their attendance too, but were in expectation that some state mine was to be sprung and somebody or other blown up, little suspecting the true matter; and for what I can hear the Court was as much surprised to find 'twas to oppose one of the ways and means of raising money. When Lowndes [Secretary of the Treasury] proposed the tax upon leather, as a certain fund that would bring in a hundred and forty thousand pounds a year, and was seconded by Mr. Benson, when he found they all rise up to oppose it he seems thunder-struck, but did bring out thus much, that as they came prepared to oppose this he hoped they had ready to offer the House in lieu thereof as good [and] valuable a fund; but they had nothing like to offer. Then the Court party called for the question, still not doubting but they should carry it, without spending any time to debate it; but they were much mistaken, for upon a division they lost it by forty. And then, when 'twas too late, Mr. St. John made them a long speech of what a fatal consequence 'twas to the affairs of the nation to refuse so good a fund for a supply, and that our credit, which was just reviving to a great height, this vote would throw it all down again. So that several politicians that could not endure Mr. Harley say they see now there's no man the Court employs has address enough to manage the House of Commons but him. If he had been well, he would either have had intelligence of what was intended, and so have endeavoured to have brought them to the House in a better temper, or at least when there he would have seen how it would have gone and would have put it off for a fitter opportunity.

But ever since, somebody has bestirred themselves and have brought the House into the temper [which] is desired; for they brought [the] business in again today by another title, a duty upon raw hides, instead of leather. For the passing of it there was 170 odd against eighty odd, which occasions much speculation how so many men in one night time should be brought over. This morning, when 'twas talked of... changing the title of the bill [as] the expedient thought of to bring it pass today, I heard some Parliament [men] say, that was by no means parliamentary, and would be an ill precedent. Yet they confess a prorogation would take up too much time, which they said was the only way to come at the bill regularly. And perhaps some have been brought to give their votes for it this way rather than be kept so long from the country, which perhaps they were told would be the consequence, for now they have voted all the supplies that have been asked.

The Wentworth Papers (ed. J. J. Cartwright, 1833), pp. 189-90

6 Tory Whips in the House of Lords, 1712

Lord Poulet to Lord Dartmouth, 'Friday morning' [29 Feb. 1712]

I went my rounds last night and found the part many friends took in the last division was more in respect to the Commons than any ill will to us [in the ministry], for they assure me this day they will vote with us; so that I have hopes from all I meet with except peevish Weymouth. I give your Lordship this account to encourage you to exert yourself, and for the credit of the service I think it must be this day debated fully. Therefore I hope you will speak to your friends, and particularly your kinsman Northampton, and that you will write to [the] Bishop of London.

William Salt Library, Stafford, Dartmouth MSS. D. 1778 V. 194

S

COURT AND COUNCIL

Some of the most decisive engagements in the conflict of parties between 1694 and 1716 were fought neither in the constituencies nor in Parliament. In order to promote the policies and defend the ideals in which they believed, the Whig and Tory leaders had to be able to influence, and if possible control, the administration as well as the legislature. A parliamentary majority for their party could not by itself ensure them a decisive voice in policy making; nor could the mere engrossment of 'places'. What mattered most of all was to win and hold the favour of the Crown and, from late in William's reign onwards, to dominate the Cabinet Council.

In the struggle for mastery in Court and Council the two parties had to contend not merely with each other but with monarchs determined not to concede complete mastery to either. William III never gave his full confidence to any set of party leaders, not even to the Whig Junto on whose services he was heavily dependent from 1694-9 (**B.2**, **ii**; **O.1**). Queen Anne recoiled from 'the merciless men of both parties' (**5**, **7**), though she had more natural sympathy with the Tories than the Whigs. Even George I would probably have preferred a middle course in 1714-15 had it been practicable for him to steer one (**10**).

A crucial factor in the relationship between the Crown and the parties up to 1714 was the role of 'the Managers' – Sunderland and Shrewsbury under King William, Godolphin, Marlborough and Robert Harley under Queen Anne. These five key post-Revolution statesmen put loyalty to the sovereign before what party allegiances, if any, they possessed; they acted as indispensable intermediaries between him and the party men; and during Anne's reign the last three were the effective heads of the executive. Their political creed was a moderate one and was rooted in distrust of party. Such a creed was not readily acceptable to men like the Junto lords, to Rochester, Seymour and Nottingham of the older Tories, or to Bromley and Bolingbroke of the younger ones. All the genuine party leaders of this period believed in what we should now call 'party government'. Not unnaturally they resented the interposition of the Managers between themselves and the undisputed control of the ministry.

From time to time they kicked against their authority, as the Junto did against the influence of Lord Sunderland in 1695 (**1**; **O.1**, **ii**). But attempts to challenge that authority outright, like that by Rochester in 1702 (**3**) or by Nottingham in 1704 (**5**), all failed; until in 1714 Bolingbroke eventually succeeded in toppling Harley (Earl of Oxford) a few days before Anne's death, only to see control of the situation pass immediately out of his hands into those of another Manager, the Duke of Shrewsbury (**9**). In the 20 years before 1714, however, the two fiercest battles to be waged at Court were fought not to achieve the unqualified supremacy of either Whig or Tory leaders, but to replace one managerial régime by another. In 1708 Harley narrowly failed to depose Godolphin and to replace the existing pattern of government with a new one of his own (**6**). In 1710, with Shrewsbury's help, he succeeded. But, in intention, neither his régime nor that of Godolphin and Marlborough involved surrender to party extremism.

Baulked of complete control, the party chiefs strove to secure, as second best, as many Cabinet seats as possible for themselves and their friends. Those in the ascendant aimed at a monopoly (**5**; **7, ii**), being convinced, as Nottingham once put it, 'that a Coalition-scheme is impracticable'.[1] Those out of favour attached the utmost importance to retaining some foothold for their party, however slight, in the Cabinet; for if nothing else, this assured them prompt access to information about government policy. Hence the perturbation of the Junto lords in 1703 at the report of Somerset's resignation from a predominantly High Tory ministry (**4**). For their own part they valued Cabinet rank, as did Rochester and Nottingham, for the influence rather than for the profit it brought them. To acquire such influence Lord Somers was prepared in 1708 to accept a place in the Cabinet without office and without emolument (**7, i**). Nottingham, on the other hand, preferred to resign his Secretaryship in 1704 rather than hold office without influence (**5**). Nor would the Hanoverian Tory leaders accept sinecures from George I in 1714 when it became plain that he was reluctant to trust them with real responsibility and authority (**10**).

Although control of the Cabinet Council, with its select membership of 10-12, was the great prize to which these men aspired, their fortunes occasionally turned on the outcome of conflict in an older arena, the Privy Council, in which the minority party usually retained a stronger representation. It was the Privy Council which advised the monarchs on the dissolution of Parliament, a vital matter of party strategy. On this issue the Whigs scored a notable victory in the Council in 1701 (**2**) and suffered a decisive defeat at the very end of their ministry in 1710.[2] In the making of war and peace, too, it was the 'Great Council' which took the final decisions. Here the High Tories made their final stand against the full commitment of England to the Spanish Succession war in 1702 (**3**); and here, eleven years later, the Whigs defended the last ditch in their fight against the Utrecht settlement. In the crisis of Queen Anne's last illness it was the fact that the Whig magnates still had the right to attend the Privy Council, at a time when the Cabinet was entirely Tory, which was probably decisive in thwarting the hopes of Bolingbroke and the Jacobites (**9**).

In the final reckoning, however, the government of England between 1694 and 1716 was still 'the King's Government' (or the Queen's).

---

[1] Leicestershire Record Office, Finch MSS. P. P. 150 (xii): paper in Nottingham's hand, n.d. [c. Feb. 1711].

[2] See *The Letters of Joseph Addison* (ed. W. Graham, 1941), pp. 239-40.

A party ascendancy in Court and Council could not long survive the withdrawal of royal confidence or favour, as the Junto found in 1699 and 1710, and the High Tories in 1704. Such favour was a precarious asset which, once lost, was not easily retrieved. Even Queen Anne was not to be browbeaten or overawed by the power-politicians, either in the privacy of the closet (**5**), or at the Cabinet table itself (a lesson the Junto learned in 1710 when they tried to frighten her away from a change of ministry by procuring the Vryberg Memorial) (**8**). It was only towards the end of Anne's reign that an opposition party, deprived of any immediate hope of power, adopted the tactic of cultivating the heir to the throne instead of its existing occupant. The endemic divisions in the Hanoverian royal family after 1714 were to make the Court an ideal field for such activities. By 1716, expelled from office, routed in the constituencies and overwhelmed in Parliament, the Tories could see only this way back into the Promised Land (**11**).

1 The King's Manager: Lord Sunderland and the Whigs, 1695

(i) The Earl of Sunderland to the Earl of Portland, 29 July 1695

Since I came hither I have met with Lord Keeper [Somers] and Lord Shrewsbury. The last will write to the King what we agreed on; of which the chief thing was to desire his Majesty would be pleased to return as soon as is possible, that the writs may go out in time for a new Parliament, taking it for granted there must be one, though Mr. Montague declares for this [present Parliament], and as I hear Mr. Wharton is of that mind, thinking they shall have less power in a new one. But I think this is unpracticable . . .

Lord Keeper and Lord Shrewsbury seem to be more my friends than ever and I believe it. I am sure of it, if they are not the falsest men alive. But I hear Wharton and Montagu have said that I must not be in the King's business, and that they can do it better without me both with the King and the Whigs. The King and you know how fond I am of being a minister. I have endeavoured hitherto to unite as many as I could to assist in the King's service, and if now I am the occasion of making differences in that party I would unite, I know nothing can make me meddle any longer. I intend to speak openly and plainly to them all and you shall know what that produces very soon.

(ii) Henry Guy to the Earl of Portland, 6 August 1695

Lord Sunderland is gone out of town this day. But before he went he hath settled all things amongst these people [the Whigs]; and all or most of them have assured him that they will be totally governed by him and will do as he shall direct. This was and is a matter of that difficulty that I will boldly say no man in England but himself could have done it ... You will easily believe this when you consider what a sort of people these are to deal with ... But ... I think it may hold, because I find they are sensible enough that they do not well know how to stir without him.

N.U.L. Portland MSS. PwA.1248, 511
[proper names have been transposed out of numerical code]

2 Cabinet and Council divided over the Dissolution of Parliament, 1701

Friedrich Bonet to Frederick III of Brandenburg, 14 November 1701 (transl.)

... On Sunday there was a meeting of the Cabinet Council, at which this question of the dissolution [of Parliament] was in the first place proposed, and then resolved upon after debates which lasted for several hours. The King afterwards revealed to several of his ministers this plan that he had formed, and among others to Lord Godolphin, who replied that if his Majesty carried it out, he would in that case beg to be allowed to resign his office; and on Tuesday, after the dissolution had been agreed on in the Great Council, he gave up his post of First Lord of the Treasury. Even in the Great Council there were still great and lengthy arguments for and against the dissolution. The Keeper of the Great Seal [Sir Nathan Wright], the President of the Council [Pembroke], the Lord Chamberlain [Jersey] and Secretary of State Hedges, among others, were strongly opposed to it. And although his Majesty made it clear that he himself wanted it, it was only decided on by a majority of three votes.

Add. MSS. 30,000 E, fo. 395

3 The Debate in the Privy Council on the Declaration of War, 1702

By this time [May 1702] there appeared to be a division among the courtiers occasioned by a rivalship about the Queen's favour between the Earls of Rochester and Marlborough. But though the great abilities, integrity and consummate experience of the former were supported by his being a near relation to her Majesty, yet the Earl of Marlborough soon got the ascendant. It having been moved in the Council to declare war against France and Spain, the Earl of Rochester and some other members represented the inconveniencies that might attend such a step, urging that it was safer for the English to act only as auxiliaries. But the Earl of Marlborough maintained, on the contrary, that it not only became the honour of the Crown and nation to make good the late King's engagements, but that France could never be reduced within due bounds unless the English entered as principals in the quarrel. This opinion being supported by the [Whig] Dukes of Somerset and Devonshire, the Earl of Pembroke and some others, the majority of that illustrious assembly gave in to it, and thereupon her Majesty ordered a declaration of war to be drawn up.

A. Boyer, *History of the Life and Reign of Queen Anne* (1722), p. 14

4 The Duke of Somerset and the Cabinet, 1703

Lord Somers to Lord Halifax, n.d. [1703]

I have heard a piece of news within this half hour which gives me inexpressible disturbance. It is that the Duke of Somerset has received a dissatisfaction occasioned by some pretences of the Lord Chamberlain [Lord Jersey] and that he is not without thoughts of quitting the Court. I am the most ignorant creature living in matters which must be the ground of such a dispute,[1] and consequently incapable of giving advice or being of any use on such an occasion; but I was so much startled at a thing which might end so fatally that I could not but resolve to come away for London immediately...

Without knowing the fact... I am partial enough to conclude the

[1] i.e. matters of Court etiquette.

Duke to be in the right; but I will take the liberty to say that, admitting him to be so, that is not enough to justify such a resolution. His quitting at this time is of too great consequence to be resolved on without an absolute necessity, I mean on such a ground that all the honest part of the kingdom [the Whigs], who respect him and think a great part of their security depends on his continuing in public business, may understand and may judge to be of moment enough ... If the occasion of his quitting be not a matter of a very public nature, somewhat wherein everybody has a concernment, it will be censured as a sort of deserting his country at so very critical [a] time, ... [and] therefore, my good Lord, bestir yourself all you can to compose this unhappy matter, as I hope all our friends will some way or other.

Add. MSS. 34521, fos. 51-2 (transcript)

5 Lord Nottingham's Ultimatum and the Fall of the High Tories, 1704

(i) The Duke of Marlborough to Lord Godolphin, Harwich, 8 April 1704

I could not leave this place without acquainting you with what has been told me concerning Lord Nottingham ... I am assured that he tells his party that the Queen is desirous to do everything that would give them satisfaction, but that she is hindered by you and me; that he is so convinced that we shall in a very short time put all the business into the hands of the Whigs, that if he can't get such alterations made in the Cabinet Council as he thinks absolutely necessary for the safety of the Church he would then quit, and that he would speak very plainly to you and myself before I left England.

Blenheim MSS. A.1-14

(ii) Lord Godolphin to the Duchess of Marlborough, Tuesday night at 11 [18 April 1704]

... I have had a very long conversation with Lord Nottingham ... There was very plain dealing on both sides, and of his side many threatenings from the Tories, intermingled with professions to me. His aim seemed to be to get the Duke of Somerset and the Archbishop [of Canterbury] out of the Cabinet Council, and Lord Carlisle out of the Lieutenancy. He was very positive that the Queen could not govern but by one party or the other, and that the keeping the duke of Som[erset] in the Cabinet Council after what had passed would render her government contemptible. I found afterwards he had given Mrs. Morley [the Queen] a good deal of these sort of notions, and she seemed to think it was not equal to displace some that had misbehaved and keep in others; but after a little talk she resolved to send her messages [of dismissal to Lord Jersey and Sir Edward Seymour] Thursday morning.

I could not be certain by Lord Nottingham's discourse whether he would quit or not. It looked all that way, but when it comes to the point I question if he will do it.

Blenheim MSS. E.20

(iii) Robert Harley to Edward Harley, 22 April 1704

... Thursday [20 April] Lord Nottingham brought the seals to the Queen: told her he could not serve her with that Cabinet, etc. She persuaded him to carry them back. This day at one a clock he hath finally delivered them. The manner of it can never be justified if he had had reasons ... The Town hath given it to Lord Sunderland or Sir William Trumbull, but mostly the latter, and he is at Bath. Yesterday Secretary Hedges went to Lord Jersey: told him the Queen found it for her service to have the staff in another hand, which greatly surprised him and everyone else, it not being talked of before. A messenger is gone down for Sir E. Seymour's [staff].

Brit. Mus. Loan 29/70/11

6 The Crisis in the Cabinet and the Fall of Harley, 1708

Jonathan Swift to Archbishop King, 12 February 1708

Yesterday the seals were taken from Mr. Harley, and Sir Thomas Mansell gave up his staff. They went to Kensington together for that purpose, and came back immediately and went together into the House of Commons. Mr. St. John designs to lay down in a few days, as a friend of his told me, though he advised him to the contrary ...

Mr. Harley had been for some time, with the greatest art imaginable, carrying on an intrigue to alter the ministry; and began with no less an enterprise than that of removing the Lord Treasurer, and had nearly effected it, by the help of Mrs. Masham, one of the Queen's dressers, who was a great and growing favourite of much industry and insinuation. It went so far that the Queen told Mr. St. John a week ago that she was resolved to part with Lord Treasurer; and sent him with a letter to the Duke of Marlborough, which she read to him, to that purpose; and she gave St. John leave to tell it about the town, which he did without any reserve; and Harley told a friend of mine a week ago that he was never safer in favour or employment.

On Sunday evening last the Lord Treasurer and Duke of Marlborough went out of the [Cabinet] Council; and Harley delivered a memorial to the Queen relating to the Emperor and the war. Upon which the Duke of Somerset rose, and said, if her Majesty suffered that fellow (pointing to Harley) to treat affairs of the war without advice of the general, he could not serve her; and so left the Council. The Earl of Pembroke,[1] though in milder words, spoke to the same purpose; so did most of the lords: and the next day the Queen was prevailed upon to turn him [Harley] out, though the seals were not delivered till yesterday ... It is said that Harley had laid a scheme for an entire new ministry, and the men are named to whom the several employments were to be given. And though his project has miscarried, it is reckoned the greatest piece of Court skill that has been acted these many years.

The Correspondence of Jonathan Swift (ed. Ball), i, 74-6

7 The Whig Junto and the Cabinet, 1708-9

(i) Queen Anne to the Duke of Marlborough, 22 April 1708

The occasion of my writing to you at this time is to give you an account of a visit I had yesterday from Lord Privy Seal and Lord Steward,[2] in which they proposed my taking Lord Somers into the Cabinet Council without giving him any employment, since I could not be prevailed upon to make him President, laying a great stress on its being necessary for my service. Their arguments did not at all convince me of the reasonableness nor the propriety of the thing. But all the answer I made was that the proposition was a very new thing, and that I thought there were enough [members] of the Cabinet Council

[1] The only other Tory by now in the Cabinet apart from Harley.
[2] The Whig Dukes of Newcastle and Devonshire.

already; that I depended upon their assistance in carrying on my business, and had no thoughts of employing any but those that served me well in the Parliament, and *had no leaning to any others*, and would countenance all that served me faithfully. This is the sense of what I said to them; and this morning I have this account to Lord Treasurer, who had heard nothing of this matter before, but joined in the two dukes' proposal, ... and I must own to you, did not convince me any more than what I had heard before on the same subject, though I have a much greater respect for him than for either of the others, looking upon it to be utter destruction to me to bring Lord Somers into my service.

> W. Coxe, *Memoirs of the Duke of Marlborough* (Bohn, 1848), ii, 219-20

(ii) James Craggs to the Duke of Marlborough, 20 May 1709

Since your Grace's departure I have had several discourses with the Junctonians, who grow more pressing in the Admiralty affair,[1] and they have now taken resolutions that the President [Lord Somers] is to speak to the Treasurer very plainly on this subject. They urge the next sessions cannot be carried on without it, for as the majority are in the Whig interest they will not be easy without being of a piece ...

To have a good majority to wind up all the bottoms of the war quietly and honourably would make this reign perfectly happy for the future and they make all these things to depend upon the good settlement of the Admiralty affairs, as the only loophole for [Tory] faction to practise upon.

> Blenheim MSS. B.1-23

8 Vryberg's Memorial, 1710

William Bromley to James Grahme, 3 July 1710

I find those among our friends that have been the greatest infidels now think ... that you will certainly have a new Parliament. The Whigs believe all this and are in the utmost rage ... They are running everywhere to make their interests. Their last effort, and on which they had great dependence, was the Dutch Letter. An handle was taken for it

---

[1] The Junto's proposal to replace the one remaining Tory in the Cabinet, Pembroke, by Lord Orford as First Lord of the Admiralty.

from [what] the [Queen] said to Mr. B[oyle, the Secretary of State] and ordered him to tell the foreign ministers upon dismissing Lord S[underland], that she did it not out of any displeasure to Lord M[arlborough], nor had she any design to remove him. Some say it was added that she did not design *aucun changement de ministre present*. This was writ by Vryberg to the States. They return thanks for this declaration, and offer it as their opinion how prejudicial any change might be to the interest of the alliance.[1] This letter was gained by the utmost importunity, and was not from the States but from the Assembly of the Week, a committee of States that sits in their absence.

The [Whig] party had advice of this letter and were strangely elated upon it; but are as much dejected upon the answer that was returned, which, as I am told, was worthy of Q. Eliz. It was given in the Cabinet without consultation upon it, and in such a manner that there was not a word offered against it.

Levens MSS.

9 The Privy Council and Anne's Last Illness

Sir John Perceval to Daniel Dering, 3 August 1714

I was at Tunbridge when the news came of her Majesty's sudden indisposition, which seized her last Friday in the head, so that she was speechless for a considerable time. Upon this the Council was summoned to meet; and accordingly not only the lords who usually attend repaired to the board, but the Whig lords, who had for some time withdrawn themselves (as you know is the custom where there are parties). They were about 40. They sat silent some time to wait the issue of the distemper. When being acquainted that her Majesty was come to herself, some lord whose name I have not yet learned moved that she might be told in the most humble manner how necessary it was in this juncture, in order to preserve the peace of her realm, that the Treasurer's staff should be conferred on some person of undoubted integrity and capacity; and then continuing, he proposed the Duke of Shrewsbury as a lord every way qualified to recommend to her.

[1] According to James Brydges, the Paymaster-General, the Memorial went even further than this. It warned the Queen that the Dutch, as guarantors of the Protestant Succession, would regard a change of ministry as a blow against Hanover and a threat that Britain might make a separate peace with France. See *Huntington Library Quarterly* (1939-40), iii, 230-1.

He had no sooner delivered his opinion but every lord there closed with it, the Lord Bolingbroke's creatures as well as the rest; and so the Lord Chancellor [was] sent in to the Queen, for they were met in an adjoining room. Immediately she sent for the Duke, and ordering the wand to be brought her, put it into his hand.

Add. MSS. 47027, pp. 292-3

10 George I and the Parties, 1714

Sir John Perceval to [Daniel Dering?], n.d. [November? 1714]

The King and royal family arrived in safety. Crowds of all ranks impatiently waited the wished-for-day, and stocks and public funds rise, and the Tories pressed with equal appearance of zeal to demonstrate their affections to his Majesty's person as could the other party...

But yet notwithstanding, the hatred which the Whigs and Tories bore one another was (as it still continues) so insurmountable that his Majesty soon became convinced of the impracticableness of taking into his intimate councils the heads of both parties. He had at his first arrival restored the Duke of Marlborough to the Generalship, the Ordnance and the Guards, which together with appointing the Earl of Sunderland Lord Lieutenant of Ireland and Stanhope Secretary of State, all 3 persons much hated by the Tory party, was very ill relished by them... They perceived the balance of his favour to lean much to the Whigs, and that he took into his service and councils such as had been particularly ill-used by themselves. They then begun to perceive that they flattered themselves in vain with the hopes of sharing in the high posts of the administration... From this time the Tories resolved to unite their strength, and if possible to gain a majority in the ensuing Parliament as the only means left to support their declining party, hoping the King might be prevailed on to dismiss his new ministers when he should be convinced that the sense of the nation ran in favour of the Church party...

I said above that the King saw within a very little while that it was impracticable to make a mixed ministry of Whig and Tory. It was to my certain knowledge his desire at first to employ those of both denominations whom he had heard a good account of, and believed true to the interest of his family, which he was very well inclined to think of many a Tory, being a wise and just man, well acquainted with the nation and not of a violent temper. But this did not satisfy the Tories. They expected places of great trust and power, and profit was not all they demanded. This the King would not consent to. He knew too well that his service could not be carried on by persons of differing principles and enemies of each other; neither had he such obligations to the Tories as to put them on an equal foot with the Whigs, who had borne the brunt of the day and eminently distinguished themselves in his service ... It is not to be imagined but that the Whigs were well pleased with these natural sentiments of the King, and laboured to confirm him in them by representing that King William owed all the troubles of his reign to a scheme with which he set out, of admitting two parties into the administration.

Add. MSS. 47027, pp. 342-8

11 The Reversionary Interest: The Prince of Wales and the Tories, 1716

Reports sent to James Stanhope, Secretary of State, August 1716

(i) From Robert Walpole, Hampton Court, 9 August

We came hither last night ... and here we find the Duke of Shrewsbury, upon pretence of the duchess's being in waiting, an inhabitant of the place, which by all accounts his public as well as private reception and conferences with both Prince and Princess sufficiently encourage. The Duke of Argyll is never absent from hence one day; he is constantly in parties of pleasure with the Prince ... You can easily conjecture what must be the consequences of these appearances. They have such an effect already as draws the Tories from all parts of the neighbourhood, gives such a disgust to the Whigs as before Michaelmas, I may venture to prophesy, the company here will be two to one of the King's enemies.

We are here chained to the oar, and working like slaves, and are looked upon as no other. For not only the behaviour and conduct of the Prince are a weight upon us, but the industrious representations that are made of our being lost with the King reduces our credit to nothing. If we are to be the King's servants, and to be supported in serving him as King, our hands must be strengthened.

(ii) From Stephen Poyntz, Hampton Court, 21 August

My Lord Townshend and Mr. Methuen . . . command me to acquaint you that they are well informed the whole body of the Tories are promoting addresses from all parts to the Prince, the heads of which they hear are already sent down, and that the general tenor of them will be to compliment the Prince upon his regency and upon showing himself disposed to be a common father to all his people, in spite of the artifices and insinuation of such as delight in war or bloodshed; by which it is intended to reflect on his Majesty's conduct, and stigmatise such of his servants as were most active in carrying on the late war against France and in pursuing the measures found necessary for suppressing the rebellion. They are assured that Sir John Pakington has undertaken to procure such an address from Worcestershire, and Mr. Bromley another from Warwickshire, and that the same are carrying on in most of the western counties . . .

My Lord Townshend and Mr. Methuen are of opinion that this is the wisest step the Jacobites have yet taken, since it manifestly tends to set up the son against the father, and to lay a lasting foundation of uneasiness and distraction among those who are best affected to the royal family. However, they think themselves obliged to do his Royal Highness the justice to declare that they neither hear, nor can perceive by any observations they have yet been able to make, that he has given the smallest encouragement to these addresses.

Coxe, Walpole, ii, 64, 75-6

Soc
DA
430
H58
1968

DATE DUE